Broadway Christian Chur...
This Momentary Marriage: A P...
Piper, John

P9-DDM-333

0000 6429

THIS MOMENTARY MARRIAGE

BOOKS BY JOHN PIPER

THIS MOMENTARY MARRIAGE

A Parable of Permanence

JOHN PIPER

CROSSWAY BOOKS
WHEATON, ILLINOIS

This Momentary Marriage

Copyright © 2009 by Desiring God Foundation

Published by Crossway Books
        a publishing ministry of Good News Publishers
        1300 Crescent Street
        Wheaton, Illinois 60187

All rights reserved. No part of this publication may be reproduced, stored in a retrieval system or transmitted in any form by any means, electronic, mechanical, photocopy, recording or otherwise, without the prior permission of the publisher, except as provided for by USA copyright law.

Cover design and illustration by: Christopher Koelle and
                          Matt Mantooth at Portland Studios, Inc.

First printing, 2009

Printed in the United States of America

Scripture quotations are taken from the ESV® Bible (*The Holy Bible: English Standard Version*®). Copyright © 2001 by Crossway Bibles, a publishing ministry of Good News Publishers. Used by permission. All rights reserved.

All emphases in Scripture quotations have been added by the author.

PDF ISBN: 978-1-4335-0713-7

MobiPocket ISBN: 978-1-4335-0714-4

Library of Congress Cataloging-in-Publication Data
Piper, John, 1946–
   This momentary marriage : a parable of permanence / John Piper.
      p. cm.
   Includes bibliographical references and indexes.
   ISBN 978-1-4335-0712-0
     1. Marriage—Religious aspects—Christianity. I. Title.
BT706.P57   2009
248.4—dc22   2009004245

LB		19	18	17	16	15	14	13	12	11	10	09
15	14	13	12	11	10	9	8	7	6	5	4	3	2	1

To

RUTH and BILL PIPER
PAMELA and GEORGE HENRY

whose marriages were broken only by death

CONTENTS

FOREWORD:
PENDULUMS AND PICTURES

Noël Piper

I know some couples who think and feel so much alike that they can work together, minister together, live together, and raise children together with hardly any conflict. Well, there might be a couple like that. But it's not us.

On personality analyses we two chart out as almost exactly opposite. According to Ruth Bell Graham, that's good. She's famous for saying that if two people agree on everything, one of them is unnecessary. But there are times I think we'd be more than willing to experiment with that kind of not being necessary.

In our real life, I swing somewhere between two extremes. At one end of the pendulum's arc, I'm in wonder: "How in the world did I get such an amazing husband? What did I ever do that he should have paid me a bit of notice, never mind that he asked me to marry him?" We took a marriage assessment during one of my blissful periods. The results placed me high on the idealism scale, recognizing few problem areas in our marriage—in other words, according to the "experts," fairly unreliable.

Somewhere on that upswing is where I wish we could stay, where there's nothing hindering our enjoyment of each other—like during one vacation in the Blue Ridge Mountains:

AWAY
Reading in rocking chair,
Butterflies and black bear,
Moss and mushrooms,

Pictures and poems,
Songs and swing,
Woodpeckers on wing,
Worship and walking,
Time for talking,
Scrabble and sleep . . .
A quiet to keep.
With you.

By contrast, when inertia and resistance are dragging us downward, I'm asking myself, "How in the world did we get into such a mess? What happened to make us feel this kind of disagreement and unhappiness?" We observed our silver anniversary during such a season:

GOING FOR GOLD

What a way to prepare for our party—
was it you who hurt me or I you?
But our smiles were constrained to seem hearty—
a veneer we were all too used to.
"May the next twenty-five be as great as
the first!" they said with their hugs and smiles,
while I tried to dream up an alias
I'd adopt after bolting for miles.
But I knew I would stay. How could I flee
the one who knew me, yet loved me still?
Then Beryl, whose years with Arnold were sixty,
matter-of-factly thawed my heart's chill.
"The years that are coming will be the best;
the first twenty-five are the hardest."

Since I apparently can't see much beyond the emotions of the moment, if we were to ask for a counselor's evaluation during those hard times, it probably would seem to reveal a marriage in trouble, a judgment just as misleading as that of idealism during days of "all's well with the world."

The pendulum of our marriage oscillates and sometimes wobbles, but it is suspended from above and is firmly attached. By God's grace, it will not crash to the ground. This year we celebrate our fortieth anniversary, and thanks to God, we feel like celebrating as we press toward the gold of our fiftieth, if God should be gracious to give us so many years.

We know it is the weight of our sin that accelerates us into the seasons at the bottom. But here's the amazing, unbelievable thing—a profound mystery, as Paul says: "'A man shall leave his father and mother and hold fast to his wife, and the two shall become one flesh.' . . . and I am saying that *it refers to Christ and the church*" (Eph. 5:31–32). Marriage refers to Christ and the church—every marriage, no matter how pendulum-like because of our sin; every marriage, even if the couple doesn't care a bit about Jesus.

To change metaphors, God designed marriage to be a picture. That makes me ask myself, how clear and well-focused is the portrait of Jesus that our marriage is displaying?

I love using my tiny digital camera. But the larger and more complex a subject, the more nearly impossible it is to represent it well and completely. No single photograph can show someone how magnificent the Grand Canyon is. It's true that my shortcomings as a photographer do nothing to change the majesty of that natural wonder. Still, some snapshots do give a better idea than others of the grandeur. I want to take that clearer kind of picture of the Grand Canyon. And that's the kind of image of Jesus I want our marriage to portray.

I pray that this book (by my favorite preacher) will focus the lenses of many marriages so that the portrait of Christ and his bride is sharp and clear.

INTRODUCTION:
MARRIAGE AND MARTYRDOM

Dietrich Bonhoeffer was engaged to be married to Maria von Wedemeyer when he was hanged at dawn on April 9, 1945, at the age of thirty-nine. As a young pastor in Germany, he had been opposed to Nazism and was finally arrested on April 5, 1943, for his involvement in a conspiracy to assassinate Adolf Hitler.

So he never married. He skipped the shadow on the way to the Reality. Some are called to one kind of display of the worth of Christ, some to another. Martyrdom, not marriage, was his calling.

Being married in the moment of death is both a sweet and bitter providence. Sweet because at the precipice of eternity the air is crystal-clear, and you see more plainly than ever the precious things that really matter about your imperfect lover. But being married at death is also bitter, because the suffering is doubled as one watches the other die, or even quadrupled if both are dying. And more if there is a child.

ONE FLESH EVEN IN DEATH

That was the case with John and Betty Stam. They were missionaries with China Inland Mission. Having met each other at Moody Bible Institute, they sailed for China separately—she in 1931, he a year later. They were married by Reuben A. Torrey on October 25, 1933, in Tsinan. John was twenty-six; Betty was twenty-seven.

The region was already dangerous because of the civil war between the Chinese Nationalist Party and the Chinese Communist Party. On September 11, 1934, Helen Priscilla was born. Three months later, her parents were beheaded by the Communists on a hill outside Miaosheo, while tiny Helen lay hidden where her mother left her with ten dollars in her blanket.

Geraldine Taylor, the daughter-in-law of Hudson Taylor (the founder of the China Inland Mission), published the story of the Stams' martyrdom two years after their death. Every time I read it, the compounding of the preciousness and the pain by the marriage and the baby make me weep.

> Never was that little one more precious than when they looked their last on her baby sweetness, as they were roughly summoned the next morning and led out to die. . . . Painfully bound with ropes, their hands behind them, stripped of their outer garments, and John barefooted (he had given Betty his socks to wear), they passed down the street where he was known to many, while the Reds shouted their ridicule and called the people to come and see the execution.
>
> Like their Master, they were led up a little hill outside the town. There, in a clump of pine trees, the Communists harangued the unwilling onlookers, too terror-stricken to utter protest—But no, one broke the ranks! The doctor of the place and a Christian, he expressed the feelings of many when he fell on his knees and pleaded for the life of his friends. Angrily repulsed by the Reds, he still persisted, until he was dragged away as a prisoner, to suffer death when it appeared that he too was a follower of Christ.
>
> John had turned to the leader of the band, asking mercy for this man. When he was sharply ordered to kneel—and the look of joy on his face, afterwards, told of the unseen Presence with them as his spirit was released—Betty was seen to quiver, but only for a moment. Bound as she was, she fell on her knees beside him. A quick command, the flash of a sword which mercifully she did not see—and they were reunited.[1]

NOTHING IS LOST

Yes, they were reunited, but not as husband and wife. For Jesus said, "When they rise from the dead, they neither marry nor are given in marriage, but are like angels in heaven" (Mark 12:25). There is no human marriage after death. The shadow of covenant-keeping between husband and wife gives way to the reality of covenant-keeping between

---

[1] Mrs. Howard Taylor, *The Triumph of John and Betty Stam* (Philadelphia: China Inland Mission, 1936), 107–108. The child had been hidden and was found by Christians and saved.

Christ and his glorified Church. Nothing is lost. The music of every pleasure is transposed into an infinitely higher key.

Dietrich Bonhoeffer and John and Betty Stam today are closer to each other in love than John and Betty Stam were, or Dietrich and Maria would have been, in marriage. They "shine like the sun in the kingdom of their Father" (Matt. 13:43). Their magnificent perfection points to the glory of Christ. And in the age to come, their bodies will be restored, and all creation will join with the children of God in everlasting joy (Rom. 8:21).

AS THE CROWN MAKES THE KING, MARRIAGE MAKES ONE

The month after Bonhoeffer's imprisonment, and two years before his death, Bonhoeffer wrote from the military section of the prison at Tegel, Berlin, "A Wedding Sermon from a Prison Cell." His text was Ephesians 1:12: ". . . so that we who were the first to hope in Christ might be to the praise of his glory."

> Marriage is more than your love for each other. . . . In your love you see only the heaven of your own happiness, but in marriage you are placed at a post of responsibility towards the world and mankind. Your love is your own private possession, but marriage is more than something personal—it is a status, and office. Just as it is the crown, and not merely the will to rule, that makes the king, so it is marriage, and not merely your love for each other, that joins you together in the sight of God and man.[2]

The aim of this book is to enlarge your vision of what marriage is. As Bonhoeffer says, it is more than your love for each other. Vastly more. Its meaning is infinitely great. I say that with care. The meaning of marriage is the display of the covenant-keeping love between Christ and his people.

This covenant-keeping love reached its climax in the death of

---

[2]Dietrich Bonhoeffer, *Letters and Papers from Prison*, ed. Eberhard Bethge (New York: Macmillan, 1967), 27. All the quotes from Bonhoeffer on the facing pages of each chapter of this book were taken from *Letters and Papers from Prison;* Dietrich Bonhoeffer, *Life Together* (London: SCM Press, 1954); Dietrich Bonhoeffer, *The Cost of Discipleship* (New York: Macmillan, 1967).

Christ for his church, his bride. That death was the ultimate expression of grace, which is the ultimate expression of God's glory, which is of infinite value. Therefore, when Paul says that our great and final destiny is "the praise of [God's] glorious grace" (Eph. 1:6), he elevates marriage beyond measure, for here, uniquely, God displays the apex of the glory of his grace: "Christ loved the church and gave himself up for her" (Eph. 5:25).

A STRANGE WAY TO START A BOOK ON MARRIAGE

Thinking about martyrdom may seem like a strange way to begin a book on marriage. If we lived in a different world, and had a different Bible, I might think it strange. But here is what I read.

> Let those who have wives live as though they had none. (1 Cor. 7:29)

> "If anyone comes to me and does not hate his own father and mother and wife and children and brothers and sisters, yes, and even his own life, he cannot be my disciple." (Luke 14:26)

> "Truly, I say to you, there is no one who has left house or wife or brothers or parents or children, for the sake of the kingdom of God, who will not receive many times more in this time, and in the age to come eternal life." (Luke 18:29–30)

I take those verses to mean: Marriage is a good gift of God, but the world is fallen, and sin abounds, and obedience is costly, and suffering is to be expected, and "a person's enemies will be those of his own household" (Matt. 10:36). High romance and passionate sexual intimacy and precious children may come. But hold them loosely—as though you were not holding them. This is what Bonhoeffer represents. To keep his life and meaning before us throughout this book, I will let him speak briefly on the facing pages at the beginning of each chapter.

Romance, sex, and childbearing are temporary gifts of God. They are not part of the next life. And they are not guaranteed even for this life. They are one possible path along the narrow way to Paradise. Marriage passes through breathtaking heights and through swamps with choking vapors. It makes many things sweeter, and with it come bitter providences.

WE MADE IT

Marriage is a momentary gift. I have only scratched the surface of its wonders and its wounds. I hope that you will go farther and deeper and higher. As this book is published, Noël and I are passing our fortieth anniversary of marriage. She is God's gift to me—far better than I deserve. We speak often of the wonder of being married till one of us dies. It has not been trouble-free. So we imagine ourselves in our seventies or eighties—when divorce is not only sin, but socially silly—sitting across from each other, perhaps at Old Country Buffet, and smiling at each other's wrinkled faces, and saying with the deepest gratitude for God's grace: "We made it."

To those who are just beginning, I simply join Dietrich Bonhoeffer in saying,

"Welcome one another . . . for the glory of God." That is God's word for your marriage. Thank him for it; thank him for leading you thus far; ask him to establish your marriage, to confirm it, sanctify it, and preserve it. So your marriage will be "for the praise of his glory." Amen.[3]

---

[3] *Letters and Papers from Prison*, 32.

As you gave the ring to one another and have now
received it a second time from the hand of the pastor,
so love comes from you, but marriage from above,
from God. As high as God is above man,
so high are the sanctity, the rights, and the promise of love.
It is not your love that sustains the marriage,
but from now on, the marriage that sustains your love.

DIETRICH BONHOEFFER,
Letters and Papers from Prison, 27–28

CHAPTER ONE

STAYING MARRIED IS NOT MAINLY ABOUT STAYING IN LOVE

Then the LORD God said, "It is not good that the man should be alone; I will make him a helper fit for him." Now out of the ground the LORD God had formed every beast of the field and every bird of the heavens and brought them to the man to see what he would call them. And whatever the man called every living creature, that was its name. The man gave names to all livestock and to the birds of the heavens and to every beast of the field. But for Adam there was not found a helper fit for him. So the LORD God caused a deep sleep to fall upon the man, and while he slept took one of his ribs and closed up its place with flesh. And the rib that the LORD God had taken from the man he made into a woman and brought her to the man. Then the man said, "This at last is bone of my bones and flesh of my flesh; she shall be called Woman, because she was taken out of Man." Therefore a man shall leave his father and his mother and hold fast to his wife, and they shall become one flesh. And the man and his wife were both naked and were not ashamed.

GENESIS 2:18–25

There never has been a generation whose general view of marriage is high enough. The chasm between the biblical vision of marriage and the common human vision is now, and has always been, gargantuan. Some cultures in history respect the importance and the permanence of marriage more than others. Some, like our own, have such low, casual, take-it-or-leave-it attitudes toward marriage as to make the biblical vision seem ludicrous to most people.

AN INCOMPREHENSIBLE VISION OF MARRIAGE

That was the case in Jesus' day as well. But ours is worse. When Jesus gave a glimpse of the magnificent view of marriage that God willed for his people, the disciples said to him, "If such is the case of a man with his wife, it is better not to marry" (Matt. 19:10). In other words, Christ's vision of the meaning of marriage was so enormously different from the disciples', they could not even imagine it to be a good thing. That such a vision could be good news was simply outside their categories.

If that was the case then—in the sober, Jewish world in which they lived—how much more will the magnificence of marriage in the mind of God seem unintelligible in a modern Western culture, where the main idol is self; and its main doctrine is autonomy; and its central act of worship is being entertained; and its three main shrines are the television, the Internet, and the cinema; and its most sacred genuflection is the uninhibited act of sexual intercourse. Such a culture will find the glory of marriage in the mind of Jesus virtually incomprehensible. Jesus would probably say to us today, when he had finished opening the mystery for us, the same thing he said in his own day: "Not everyone can receive this saying, but only those to whom it is given. . . . Let the one who is able to receive this receive it" (Matt. 19:11–12).

WAKING UP FROM THE CULTURAL MIRAGE

So I start with the assumption that my own sin and selfishness and cultural bondage makes it almost impossible for me to feel the wonder of God's purpose for marriage. The fact that we live in a society that can defend two men or two women entering a sexual relationship and, with wild inconceivability, call it *marriage* shows that the collapse of our culture into debauchery and anarchy is probably not far away.

I mention this cultural distortion of marriage in the hopes that it might wake you up to consider a vision of marriage higher and deeper and stronger and more glorious than anything this culture—or perhaps you yourself—ever imagined. The greatness and glory of marriage is beyond our ability to think or feel without divine revelation and without the illumining and awakening work of the Holy Spirit. The world cannot know what marriage is without learning it from God. The natural man does not have the capacities to see or receive or feel the wonder of what God has designed for marriage to be. I pray that this book might be used by God to help set you free from small, worldly, culturally contaminated, self-centered, Christ-ignoring, God-neglecting, romance-intoxicated, unbiblical views of marriage.

The most foundational thing to see from the Bible about marriage is that it is God's doing. And the ultimate thing to see from the Bible about marriage is that it is for God's glory. Those are the two points I have to make. Most *foundationally*, marriage is the *doing* of God. And *ultimately*, marriage is the *display* of God.

1. MARRIAGE IS GOD'S DOING

First, most foundationally, marriage is God's doing. There are at least four ways to see this explicitly or implicitly in Genesis 2:18–25.

a) Marriage Was God's Design

Marriage is God's doing because it was his design in the creation of man as male and female. This was made plain earlier in Genesis 1:27–28: "God created man in his own image, in the image of God he created him; male and female he created them. And God blessed them. And God said to them, 'Be fruitful and multiply and fill the earth.'"

But it is also clear here in the flow of thought in Genesis 2. In verse 18, it is God himself who decrees that man's solitude is not good, and it is God himself who sets out to complete one of the central designs of creation, namely, man and woman in marriage. "It is not good that the man should be alone; *I will make him a helper fit for him.*" Don't miss that central and all-important statement: God himself will make a being perfectly suited for him—a wife.

Then he parades the animals before Adam so that he might see there is no creature that qualifies. This creature must be made uniquely from man so that she will be of his essence—a fellow human being in God's image, just as Genesis 1:27 said. So we read in verses 21–22, "So the LORD God caused a deep sleep to fall upon the man, and while he slept took one of his ribs and closed up its place with flesh. And the rib

that the LORD God had taken from the man he made into a woman."
God made her.

This text ends in verses 24–25 with the words, "They shall become one flesh. And the man and his wife were both naked and were not ashamed." In other words, this is all moving toward marriage. So the first thing to say about marriage being God's doing is that marriage was his design in creating man male and female.

b) God Gave Away the First Bride

Marriage is also God's doing because he took the role of being the first Father to give away the bride. Genesis 2:22: "And the rib that the LORD God had taken from the man he made into a woman and *brought her to the man*." He didn't hide her and make Adam seek. He made her; then he brought her. In a profound sense, he had fathered her. And now, though she was his by virtue of creation, he gave her to the man in this absolutely new kind of relationship called *marriage*, unlike every other relationship in the world.

c) God Spoke the Design of Marriage into Existence

Marriage is God's doing because God not only created the woman with this design and brought her to the man like a father brings his daughter to her husband, but also because God spoke the design of marriage into existence. He did this in verse 24: "Therefore a man shall leave his father and his mother and hold fast to his wife, and they shall become one flesh."

Who is talking in verse 24? The writer of Genesis is talking. And what did Jesus believe about the writer of Genesis? He believed it was Moses (Luke 24:44). He also believed that Moses was inspired by God, so that what Moses was saying, God was saying. We can see this if we look carefully at Matthew 19:4–5: "[Jesus] answered, 'Have you not read that he [God] who created them from the beginning made them male and female, and *said* [Note: *God* said!], "Therefore a man shall leave his father and his mother and hold fast to his wife, and the two shall become one flesh"'?" Jesus said that the words of Genesis 2:24 are God's words, even though they were written by Moses.

Therefore, marriage is God's doing because God spoke the earliest design of it into existence—"A man shall leave his father and his mother and hold fast to his wife, and they shall become one flesh."

d) God Performs the One-Flesh Union

The fourth way that marriage is God's doing is seen in the fact that God himself performs the union referred to in the words "become one flesh." That union is at the heart of what marriage is.

Genesis 2:24 is God's word of institution for marriage. But just as it was God who took the woman from the flesh of man (Gen. 2:21), it is God who in each marriage ordains and performs a uniting called *one flesh*. Man does not create this. God does. And it is not in man's power to destroy. This is implicit here in Genesis 2:24, but Jesus makes it explicit in Mark 10:8–9. He quotes Genesis 2:24, then adds a comment that explodes like thunder with the glory of marriage. "'The two shall become one flesh.' So they are no longer two but one flesh. *What therefore God has joined together, let not man separate.*"

When a couple speaks their vows, it is not a man or a woman or a pastor or parent who is the main actor—the main doer. God is. God joins a husband and a wife into a one-flesh union. *God* does that. The world does not know this. Which is one of the reasons why marriage is treated so casually. And Christians often *act* like they don't know it, which is one of the reasons marriage in the church is not seen as the wonder it is. Marriage is God's doing because it is a one-flesh union that God himself performs.

So, in sum, the most foundational thing we can say about marriage is that it is God's doing. It's his doing:

> a. because it was his design in creation;
> b. because he personally gave away the first bride in marriage;
> c. because he spoke the design of marriage into existence: leave parents, hold fast to your wife, become one flesh;
> d. and because this one-flesh union is established by God himself in each marriage.

A glimpse into the magnificence of marriage comes from seeing in

God's word that God himself is the great doer. Marriage is his doing. It is *from* him and *through* him. That is the most *foundational* thing we can say about marriage.

Now we turn to the most ultimate thing we can say about marriage. It is not only *from* him and *through* him. It is also *for* him.

2. MARRIAGE IS FOR GOD'S GLORY

The *ultimate* thing to see in the Bible about marriage is that it exists for God's glory. Most foundationally, marriage is the *doing* of God. Most ultimately, marriage is the *display* of God. It is designed by God to display his glory in a way that no other event or institution does.

The way to see this most clearly is to connect Genesis 2:24 with its use in Ephesians 5:31–32. In Genesis 2:24, God says, "Therefore a man shall leave his father and his mother and hold fast to his wife, and they shall become one flesh." What kind of relationship is this? How are these two people held together? Can they walk away from this relationship? Can they go from spouse to spouse? Is this relationship rooted in romance? Sexual desire? Need for companionship? Cultural convenience? What is this? What holds it together?

THE MYSTERY OF MARRIAGE REVEALED

In Genesis 2:24, the words "*hold fast* to his wife" and the words "they shall *become one flesh*" point to something far deeper and more permanent than serial marriages and occasional adultery. What these words point to is marriage as a sacred *covenant* rooted in covenant commitments that stand against every storm "as long as we both shall live." But that is only implicit here. It becomes explicit when the mystery of marriage is more fully revealed in Ephesians 5:31–32.

Paul quotes Genesis 2:24 in verse 31: "Therefore a man shall leave his father and mother and hold fast to his wife, and the two shall become one flesh." Then he gives it this all-important interpretation in verse 32: "This mystery is profound, and I am saying that it refers to Christ and the church." In other words, marriage is patterned after Christ's covenant commitment to his church.

Christ thought of himself as the bridegroom coming for his bride, the true people of God (Matt. 9:15; 25:1ff.; John 3:29). Paul knew his ministry was to gather the bride—the true people of God who would trust Christ. His calling was to betroth the church to her husband, Jesus. Paul puts it like this in 2 Corinthians 11:2: "I feel a divine jealousy for you, since I betrothed you to one husband, to present you as a pure virgin to Christ."

Christ knew he would have to pay for his bride with his own blood. He called this relationship the *new covenant*—"This cup that is poured out for you is the new covenant in my blood" (Luke 22:20). This is what Paul is referring to when he says that marriage is a great mystery: "I am saying that it refers to Christ and the church." Christ obtained the church by his blood and formed a new covenant with her, an unbreakable "marriage."

The ultimate thing we can say about marriage is that it exists for God's glory. That is, it exists to display God. Now we see how: Marriage is patterned after Christ's covenant relationship to his redeemed people, the church. And therefore, the highest meaning and the most ultimate purpose of marriage is to put the covenant relationship of Christ and his church on display. That is why marriage exists. If you are married, that is why you are married. If you hope to be, that should be your dream.

CHRIST WILL NEVER LEAVE HIS WIFE

Staying married, therefore, is not mainly about staying in love. It is about keeping covenant. "Till death do us part" or "As long as we both shall live" is a sacred covenant promise—the same kind Jesus made with his bride when he died for her. Therefore, what makes divorce and remarriage so horrific in God's eyes is not merely that it involves covenant-breaking to the spouse, but that it involves misrepresenting Christ and his covenant. Christ will never leave his wife. Ever. There may be times of painful distance and tragic backsliding on our part. But Christ keeps his covenant forever. Marriage is a display of that! That is the ultimate thing we can say about it. It puts the glory of Christ's covenant-keeping love on display.

The most important implication of this conclusion is that keeping covenant with our spouse is as important as telling the truth about

God's covenant with us in Jesus Christ. Marriage is not mainly about being or staying in love. It's mainly about telling the truth with our lives. It's about portraying something true about Jesus Christ and the way he relates to his people. It is about showing in real life the glory of the gospel.

Jesus died for sinners. He forged a covenant in the white-hot heat of his suffering in our place. He made an imperfect bride his own with the price of his blood and covered her with the garments of his own righteousness. He said, "I am with you . . . to the end of the age. . . . I will never leave you nor forsake you" (Matt. 28:20; Heb. 13:5). Marriage is meant by God to put that gospel reality on display in the world. That is why we are married. That is why all married people are married, even when they don't know and embrace this gospel.

PROPERTY OF
BROADWAY CHRISTIAN CHURCH LIBRARY
910 BROADWAY
FORT WAYNE, IN 46802

Over the destiny of woman and of man lies the dark shadow of a word of God's wrath, a burden from God, which they must carry. The woman must bear her children in pain, and in providing for his family the man must reap many thorns and thistles, and labor in the sweat of his brow. This burden should cause both man and wife to call on God, and should remind them of their eternal destiny in his kingdom. Earthly society is only the beginning of the heavenly society, the earthly home an image of the heavenly home, the earthly family a symbol of the fatherhood of God.

DIETRICH BONHOEFFER,
Letters and Papers from Prison, 31

CHAPTER TWO

NAKED AND NOT ASHAMED

And the man and his wife were both naked and were not ashamed.

GENESIS 2:25

Marriage is more wonderful than anyone on earth knows. The reasons it is wonderful can be learned only from God's special revelation and can be cherished only by the work of the Holy Spirit to enable us to behold and embrace the wonder. The reason we need the Spirit's help is that the wonder of marriage is woven into the wonder of the gospel of the cross of Christ, and the message of the cross is foolishness to the natural man, and so the meaning of marriage is foolishness to the natural man (1 Cor. 2:14).

For example, the well-known atheist Richard Dawkins said in an interview in 2006,

> I provided . . . cogent arguments against a supernatural intelligent designer. But it does seem to me to be a worthy idea. Refutable—but nevertheless grand and big enough to be worthy of respect. I don't see the Olympian gods or Jesus coming down and dying on the Cross as worthy of that grandeur. They strike me as parochial.[1]

These are the tragic words of "the natural man." Those who regard Christ and his incarnation and death and resurrection and lordship over all the universe as parochial cannot see the wonder of the gospel woven into marriage. In fact, Jesus is not parochial. He created the universe (John 1:3; Col. 1:16). He upholds it by the word of his power (Heb.

---

[1] "God vs. Science: An Interview with Francis Collins and Richard Dawkins," *Time*, August 5, 2006, http://www.time.com/time/magazine/article/0,9171,1555132-9,00.html; accessed 05-05-08.

1:3). The universe was created for him (Col. 1:16), and all of reality finds its highest reason for being in relation to the greatest display of the glory of God in the universe—namely, the glory of his grace supremely manifest in the death of Christ to bring sinners to God (Eph. 1:6). Only the blind call Christ and his redeeming work parochial.

But by God's grace, even Dawkins might see the glory of Christ in the gospel and in its portrayal in marriage. It is a miracle that any of us has seen this glory in the gospel. God alone can "give the light of the knowledge of the glory of God in the face of Jesus Christ" (2 Cor. 4:6). I pray that God will reveal the glory of the gospel and the meaning of marriage to Richard Dawkins—and to you. I believe he will do so for you, if you will look steadfastly at the revelation of it in God's word and seek the help of God's Spirit to enable you to see and savor the glory of Christ and his blood-bought covenant with the church, which is reflected in marriage.

MARRIAGE IS THE *DOING* OF GOD, TO THE *GLORY* OF GOD

In the previous chapter, we saw that the most *fundamental* thing we can say about marriage is that it is the *doing* of God. And the *ultimate* thing we can say about marriage is that it is the *display* of God. The reason it is the display of God is that in Christ, God has made a new covenant with his people. In it he promises to forgive and justify and glorify all who turn to him from sin and receive Christ as the Savior and Lord and supreme Treasure of their lives. Marriage between a man and a woman was designed from the beginning to be a reflection and display of that blood-bought covenant relationship.

That's why Paul quotes Genesis 2:24—"A man shall leave his father and mother and hold fast to his wife, and the two shall become one flesh"—and then says, "This mystery is profound, and I am saying that it refers to Christ and the church" (Eph. 5:31–32). Leaving parents and holding fast to a wife, forming a new one-flesh union, is meant from the beginning to display this new covenant—Christ's leaving his Father and taking the church as his bride, at the cost of his life, and holding fast to her in a one-spirit union forever.

"One spirit" is the way Paul describes the counterpart to "one flesh" in 1 Corinthians 6:16–17. He happens to be addressing the problem of prostitution, not marriage. He is arguing that our union with Christ makes union with a prostitute unthinkable. He says,

> Do you not know that your bodies are members of Christ? Shall I then take the members of Christ and make them members of a prostitute? Never! Or do you not know that he who is joined to a prostitute becomes one body with her? For, as it is written, "The two will become one flesh." But he who is joined to the Lord becomes one spirit with him. (1 Cor. 6:15–17)

I don't think Paul means that a man is married to every prostitute with whom he ever had sex. Jesus said to the woman who had had "five husbands" that "the one you now have is not your husband" (John 4:18). In other words, sex by itself did not make a marriage.

Prostitution, as the name implies, is an exploitation of marriage prerogatives. As such it plays with sacred depths. Paul uses the language of "one body" and "one flesh" to show the utter betrayal of what these phrases are meant to signify.

He is saying: You are desecrating the act of sexual union. It has the meaning of "one flesh" and "one body" *in marriage*—something profound and spiritual. But you are implicitly expressing that sacred truth with a prostitute. The shell of oneness is there, but not the covenant meaning.

The main point here is simply that in Paul's mind the covenant union between a husband and wife is designed by God to reflect and display the spiritual union between Christ and the church. So he says, "He who is joined to the Lord becomes one spirit with him."

So I argue that staying married is not mainly about staying in love. It's about covenant-keeping. If a spouse falls in love with another person, one profoundly legitimate response from the grieved spouse and from the church is, "So what! Your being 'in love' with someone else is not decisive. Keeping your covenant is decisive."

Now it is time to probe more deeply into what this covenant-keeping looks like and what it means.

NAKED AND NOT ASHAMED

To lay a deeper foundation for marriage from God's word, we turn to a key verse that we passed over in the previous chapter, namely, Genesis 2:25. After saying in verse 24, "A man shall leave his father and his mother and hold fast to his wife, and they shall become one flesh," the writer says in verse 25, "And the man and his wife were both naked and were not ashamed." What is the point of that verse?

Consider these two possible reasons why they were not ashamed. First is the reason that they both had perfect bodies. Remember, this was before the fall of creation into sin and futility. These were the very bodies that God himself had made. Therefore, since their appearance was perfect, they did not have the slightest fear that their spouse would disapprove of them. In other words, their freedom from shame was because they had absolutely nothing to be ashamed of. Is that the main point?

It is certainly a true observation. When God created man, he said that his creation was "very good" (Gen. 1:31). So the man and the woman were perfectly beautiful and handsome. There was no flaw and no blemish. Is that the point of Genesis 2:25? I doubt it. For three reasons.

NOT BECAUSE OF PERFECT BODIES

First, no matter how beautiful or handsome your spouse is, if you're cranky or selfish or unkind, you can make comments in a way that shames the other person. Not being ashamed in a marriage relationship takes more than being physically perfect; the one who is looking at you must be morally upright and gracious. Otherwise he or she can find a way to shame you. So mere physical perfection would not be enough to eliminate the possibility of being shamed.

Second, Genesis 2:24–25 is intended to provide foundational wisdom for marriage long after the fall of man into sin. We can see this by the way Jesus makes use of verse 24. He makes it the basis of his statement, "What therefore God has joined together, let not man separate" (Mark 10:9). In other words, what God is revealing in Genesis 2:24–25 has relevance long after the Fall. So it doesn't seem that the main point would only relate to the pre-Fall situation, namely, the perfection of their bodies.

Third, verse 24 (holding fast in a one-flesh union) creates the relationship where verse 25 (naked and not ashamed) can happen. And the emphasis falls there on the covenant commitment in verse 24: These two are holding fast to each other in a new one-flesh union that is not an experiment. It's a new kind of lasting union rooted in a covenant commitment. That is what creates the context for a shame-free marriage—not their perfect beauty.

BECAUSE OF COVENANT LOVE

Consider a second possibility for why they are naked and not ashamed. My suggestion is that the emphasis falls *not* on their freedom from physical imperfection, but on the fullness of covenant love. In other words, I can be free from shame for two conceivable reasons: One conceivable (but unreal) reason is that I am perfect and have nothing to be ashamed of. The other reason I could be free from shame is that even though I am imperfect, I have no fear of being disapproved by my spouse.

The first way to be shame-free is to be perfect; the second way to be shame-free is based on the gracious nature of covenant love. In the first case, there is no shame because we're flawless. In the second case, there is no shame because covenant love covers a multitude of flaws (1 Peter 4:8; 1 Cor. 13:6).

I know that in Genesis 2:25 the fall into sin has not yet happened. So there are no flaws to be covered. But my point is that verse 25 flows out of verse 24 because the covenant relationship established by marriage is designed from the beginning to be the main foundation of freedom from shame. Admittedly, until sin came into the world and all kinds of physical and moral flaws came with it, Adam and Eve did not have to exercise their covenant love to cover any sins and flaws in each other. But the eventual exercise of that covenant love *was* God's design.

Marriage was designed from the beginning to display the new covenant between Christ and the church. We have seen this in Ephesians 5:31–32. The very essence of this new covenant is that Christ passes over the sins of his bride. His bride is free from shame *not* because she is perfect, but because she has no fear that her lover will condemn her or shame her because of her sin.

This is why the doctrine of justification by grace through faith is at the very heart of what makes marriage work the way God designed it. Justification creates peace with God vertically, in spite of our sin. And when experienced horizontally, it creates shame-free peace between an imperfect man and an imperfect woman. I hope to look more fully at this in the next chapter.

DECLARING INDEPENDENCE

But first we need to finish looking at what Genesis 2 and 3 have to say about nakedness and shame. In Genesis 2:17, God had said to Adam, "Of the tree of the knowledge of good and evil you shall not eat, for in the day that you eat of it you shall surely die." I take "the knowledge of good and evil" to refer to a status of independence from God in which Adam and Eve would decide for themselves apart from God what is good and what is evil. So eating from this tree would mean a declaration of independence from God.

In Genesis 3:5–6, that is what happens:

> [The tempter says,] "God knows that when you eat of it your eyes will be opened, and you will be like God, knowing good and evil." So when the woman saw that the tree was good for food, and that it was a delight to the eyes, and that the tree was to be desired to make one wise, she took of its fruit and ate, and she also gave some to her husband who was with her, and he ate.

The first effect of this rebellion against God and this declaration of independence is recorded in verse 7: "Then the eyes of both were opened, and they knew that they were naked. And they sewed fig leaves together and made themselves loincloths." What does this mean?

Suddenly they are self-conscious about their bodies. Before their rebellion against God there was no shame. Now, evidently, there is shame. Why? There is no reason to think it's because they suddenly became ugly. That's not the focus of the text at all. Their beauty wasn't the focus in Genesis 2:25, and their ugliness is not the focus here in

Genesis 3:7. Why then the shame? Because the foundation of covenant-keeping love collapsed. And with it the sweet, all-trusting security of marriage disappeared forever.

THE FOUNDATION OF COVENANT-KEEPING LOVE

The foundation of covenant-keeping love between a man and a woman is the unbroken covenant between them and God—God governing them for their good and they enjoying him in that security and relying on him. When they ate from the tree of the knowledge of good and evil, that covenant was broken, and the foundation of their own covenant-keeping collapsed.

They experienced this immediately in the corruption of their own covenant love for each other. It happened in two ways. And we experience it today in these same two ways. Both relate to the experience of shame. In the first case, the person viewing my nakedness is no longer trustworthy, so I am afraid I will be shamed. In the second, I myself am no longer at peace with God, and I feel guilty and defiled and unworthy—I deserve to be shamed. Let's think about these one at a time.

VULNERABILITY TO SHAME

In the first case, I am self-conscious of my body and I feel vulnerable to shame because I know Eve has chosen to be independent from God. She has made herself central in the place of God. She is essentially now a selfish person. From this day forward, she will put herself first. She is no longer a servant. So she is not safe. And I feel vulnerable around her, because she is very likely to put me down if that puts her up. So suddenly my nakedness is precarious. I don't trust her anymore to love me with pure, covenant-keeping love. That's one source of shame and self-consciousness.

THE BROKEN COVENANT WITH GOD

The other source is that Adam himself, not just his spouse, has broken covenant with God. If she is rebellious and selfish, and therefore unsafe, so am I. But the way I experience it in myself is that I feel defiled and guilty and unworthy. That's, in fact, what I am. Before the Fall, what *was* and what *ought to have been* were the same. But now, what *is* and what *ought to be* are not the same.

I ought to be humbly and gladly submissive to God. But I am not. This huge gap between what I *am* and what I *ought to be* colors everything about me—including how I feel about my body. So my wife might be the safest person in the world, but now my own sense of guilt and unworthiness makes me feel vulnerable. The simple, open nakedness of innocence now feels inconsistent with the guilty person that I am. I feel ashamed.

So the shame of nakedness arises from two sources, and both of them are owing to the collapse of the foundation of covenant love in our relationship with God. One is that Eve is no longer reliable to cherish me; she has become selfish and I feel vulnerable to her putting me down for her own selfish ends. The other is that I already know that I am guilty myself, and the nakedness of innocence contradicts my unworthiness—I am ashamed.

THEY CLOTHED THEMSELVES

Genesis 3:7 says that they tried to cope with this new situation by making clothing: "And they sewed fig leaves together and made themselves loincloths." Then in Genesis 3:21, God made better clothes for them from animal skins: "And the LORD God made for Adam and for his wife garments of skins and clothed them." What are we to make of this?

Adam's and Eve's effort to clothe themselves was a sinful effort to conceal what had really happened. They tried to hide from God (Gen. 3:8). They were no longer innocent but were rebels against God. Their nakedness felt too revealing and too vulnerable. So they tried to close the gap between what they were and what they ought to be by covering what is and presenting themselves in a new way. From their standpoint, this was the origin of hypocrisy. It was the first attempted—and totally unsuccessful—snow job.

THEN GOD CLOTHED THEM

So what does it mean that God clothed them with animal skins? Was he confirming their hypocrisy? Was he aiding and abetting their pretense?

If they were naked and shame-free before the Fall, and if they put on clothes to minimize their shame after the Fall, then what is God doing by clothing them even better than they can clothe themselves? I think the answer is that he is doing something with a negative message and something with a positive message.

Negatively, he is saying: You are not what you were, and you are not what you ought to be. The chasm between what you are and what you ought to be is huge. Covering yourself with clothing is a right response to this—not to conceal it, but to confess it. Henceforth, you shall wear clothing, not to conceal that you are not what you should be, but to confess that you are not what you should be. One practical implication of this is that public nudity today is not a return to innocence but rebellion against moral reality. God ordains clothes to witness to the glory we have lost, and it is added rebellion to throw them off.[2]

And for those who rebel in the other direction and make clothes themselves a means of power and prestige and attention-getting, God's answer is not a return to nudity but a return to simplicity (1 Tim. 2:9–10; 1 Peter 3:4–5). Clothes are not meant to make people think about what is under the clothes. Clothes are meant to direct attention to what is *not* under them: merciful *hands* that serve others in the name of Christ, beautiful *feet* that carry the gospel where it is needed, and the brightness of a *face* that has beheld the glory of Jesus.

THE SIGNIFICANCE OF CLOTHING

Now we have already crossed over to the more positive meaning of clothing that God had in his mind when he clothed Adam and Eve with animal skins. This was not only a witness to the glory we lost and a confession that we are not what we should be, but it is also a testimony that God himself would one day make us what we should be. God rejected

---

[2]In response to the question about cultures where nudity is normal, I would say two things. One is that there is a measure of relativism in what is considered modest or lewd from culture to culture. Second, total nudity as a norm is very rare among the cultures of the world. In view of what happens in Genesis 3, I would say that this state of "normalcy" in these rare cultures is not a sign of innocence or divine approval but of disorder. As they are brought into a fuller knowledge of God and his word, what felt normal will not continue to feel normal, and I don't think this will simply be owing to Western imposition.

their own self-clothing. Then he clothed them himself. He showed mercy with superior clothing.

Together with the other hopeful signs in the context (like the defeat of the serpent in Gen. 3:15), God's mercy points to the day when he will solve the problem of our shame decisively and permanently. He will do it with the blood of his own Son (as there was apparently blood shed in the killing of the animals of the skins). And he will do it with the clothing of righteousness and the radiance of his glory (Gal. 3:27; Phil. 3:21).

Which means that our clothes are a witness both to our past and present failure and to our future glory. They testify to the chasm between what we are and what we should be. And they testify to God's merciful intention to bridge that chasm through Jesus Christ and his death for our sins. He will solve the problem of fear and pride and selfishness and shame between man and woman with his new blood-bought covenant.

Amazingly in the very context of the collapse of the covenant between God and man, and the collapse of the marriage covenant between Adam and Eve, God points by his mercy to the redemption that marriage itself is designed to display. God's design for marriage as a display of covenant-keeping *mercy* was not an afterthought. After the Fall, God did not have to redesign marriage. He knew what he had created in Genesis 2:24. And he knew what would happen in Genesis 3. The design of marriage, the fall of marriage, and the implied redemption of marriage all serve to tell us what marriage is for. Marriage exists to display the merciful covenant-keeping love of Christ and the faithfulness of his bride.

What we turn to, therefore, in the next chapter is the question of how a husband and a wife embody the new-covenant gospel of justification by faith alone and so create a safe and sacred place where it can be said again, "They were both naked and were not ashamed."

Their fellowship is founded solely upon Jesus Christ and this "alien righteousness." All we can say, therefore, is: the community of Christians springs solely from the biblical and Reformation message of the justification of man through grace alone; this alone is the basis of the longing of Christians for one another.

DIETRICH BONHOEFFER,
Life Together, 12

In a word, live together in the forgiveness of your sins, for without it no human fellowship, least of all a marriage, can survive.

DIETRICH BONHOEFFER,
Letters and Papers from Prison, 31

CHAPTER THREE

GOD'S SHOWCASE OF COVENANT-KEEPING GRACE

And you, who were dead in your trespasses and the uncircumcision of your flesh, God made alive together with him, having forgiven us all our trespasses, by canceling the record of debt that stood against us with its legal demands. This he set aside, nailing it to the cross. He disarmed the rulers and authorities and put them to open shame, by triumphing over them in him. . . . Put on then, as God's chosen ones, holy and beloved, compassionate hearts, kindness, humility, meekness, and patience, bearing with one another and, if one has a complaint against another, forgiving each other; as the Lord has forgiven you, so you also must forgive. And above all these put on love, which binds everything together in perfect harmony. And let the peace of Christ rule in your hearts, to which indeed you were called in one body. And be thankful. Let the word of Christ dwell in you richly, teaching and admonishing one another in all wisdom, singing psalms and hymns and spiritual songs, with thankfulness in your hearts to God. And whatever you do, in word or deed, do everything in the name of the Lord Jesus, giving thanks to God the Father through him. Wives, submit to your husbands, as is fitting in the Lord. Husbands, love your wives, and do not be harsh with them.

COLOSSIANS 2:13–15; 3:12–19

What we have seen in the last two chapters is that the most foundational thing you can say about marriage is that it is the *doing of God*, and the ultimate thing you can say about marriage is that it is for the *display of God*. These two points are made by Moses in Genesis 2. But they are made even more clearly by Jesus and Paul in the New Testament.

JESUS: MARRIAGE IS THE *DOING* OF GOD

Jesus makes the point most clearly that marriage is the *doing of God.* Mark 10:6–9:

> "From the beginning of creation, 'God made them male and female' [Genesis 1:27], 'Therefore a man shall leave his father and mother and hold fast to his wife, and the two shall become one flesh' [Genesis 2:24]. So they are no longer two but one flesh. What therefore *God has joined together*, let not man separate."

This is the clearest statement in the Bible that marriage is not merely a human doing. The words "God has joined together" means it is *God's* doing.

PAUL: MARRIAGE IS THE *DISPLAY* OF GOD

Paul makes the point most clearly that marriage is designed to be the *display of God.* In Ephesians 5:31–32 he quotes Genesis 2:24 and then tells us the mystery that it has always contained: "'Therefore a man shall leave his father and mother and hold fast to his wife, and the two shall become one flesh.' This mystery is profound, and I am saying that it refers to Christ and the church."

In other words, the covenant involved in leaving mother and father and holding fast to a spouse and becoming one flesh is a portrayal of the covenant between Christ and his church. Marriage exists ultimately to display the covenant-keeping love between Christ and his church.

A MODEL OF CHRIST AND THE CHURCH

I asked my wife Noël if there was anything she wanted me to say at this point when I was preaching on this subject. She said, "You cannot say too often that marriage is a model of Christ and the church." I think she is right, and there are at least three reasons: 1) This lifts marriage out of the sordid sitcom images and gives it the magnificent meaning God meant it to have; 2) this gives marriage a solid basis in grace, since Christ obtained and sustains his bride by grace alone; and 3) this shows that the husband's headship and the wife's submission are *crucial* and *crucified.* That is, they are woven into the very meaning of marriage as a display of Christ and the church, but they are both defined by Christ's self-denying work on the cross so that their pride and slavishness are canceled.

We spent the first two chapters on the first of these reasons: giving the foundation for marriage as a display of the covenant love of God. Marriage is a covenant between a man and a woman in which they promise to be a faithful husband and a faithful wife in a new one-flesh union as long as they both shall live. This covenant, sealed with solemn vows, is designed to showcase the covenant-keeping grace of God.

A SOLID BASIS IN GRACE

The title of this chapter is "God's Showcase of Covenant-Keeping Grace." So we are turning to the second reason I mentioned that Noël is right to say that you can't say too often that marriage is a model of Christ and the church—namely, that this gives marriage a solid basis in grace, since Christ obtained and sustains his bride by grace alone.

In other words, the main point in this chapter is that since Christ's new covenant with his church is created by and sustained by blood-bought grace, therefore, human marriages are meant to showcase that new-covenant grace. And the way husbands and wives showcase it is by resting in the experience of God's grace and bending it out from a vertical experience with God into a horizontal experience with their spouse. In other words, in marriage you live hour by hour in glad dependence on God's forgiveness and justification and promised future grace, and you bend it out toward your spouse hour by hour—as an extension of God's forgiveness and justification and promised help.

THE CENTRALITY OF FORGIVING, JUSTIFYING GRACE

I am aware that all Christians, not just married ones, are supposed to do this in all our relationships. All of us, married and single, are supposed to live hour by hour by the forgiving, justifying, all-supplying grace of God and then bend it out to all the others in our lives. Jesus says that all of life, not just marriage, is a showcase of God's glory. "Let your light shine before others, so that they may see your good works and give glory to your Father who is in heaven" (Matt. 5:16). Paul makes the same point: "Whether you eat or drink, or whatever you do, do all to the glory of God" (1 Cor. 10:31). All of life, not just marriage, is meant to showcase the glory of God, including the glory of his all-satisfying grace.

But marriage is designed to be a *unique* display of God's covenant grace because, unlike all other human relationships, the husband and wife are bound by covenant into the closest possible relationship for a lifetime. There are unique roles of headship and submission. Those distinct roles are not the focus in this chapter. That will come later.[1] Here I want to consider husband and wife simply as *Christians*. Before a man and woman can live out the unique roles of headship and submission in a biblical and gracious way, they must experience what it means to build their lives on the vertical experience of God's forgiveness and justification and promised help, and then bend it out horizontally to their spouse. That's the focus in this chapter.

Or to put it in the terms of the previous chapter: The key to being naked and not ashamed (Gen. 2:25)—when, in fact, a husband and a wife do many things that they should be ashamed of—is the experience of God's vertical forgiving, justifying grace bent out horizontally to each other and displayed to the world.

IS THE WRATH OF GOD RELEVANT FOR MARRIAGE?

Briefly, let's see the foundation for this truth in Colossians. We will start with Colossians 3:6: "On account of these the wrath of God is coming." If you say, "The last thing I want to hear about in my troubled marriage is the wrath of God," you are like a frustrated fisherman on the western coast of Indonesia on December 26, 2004, saying, "The last thing I want to hear about in my troubled fishing business is a tsunami."

A profound understanding and fear of God's wrath is exactly what many marriages need, because without it, the gospel is diluted down to mere human relations and loses its biblical glory. Without a biblical

---

[1] See Chapters 6–8.

view of God's wrath, you will be tempted to think that *your* wrath—
your anger—against your spouse is simply too big to overcome, because
you have never really tasted what it is like to see an infinitely greater
wrath overcome by grace, namely, God's wrath against you.

So we begin with the wrath of God and its removal. In Colossians
2:13–14, Paul writes one of the most wonderful things imaginable:

> And you, who were dead in your trespasses and the uncircumcision
> of your flesh, God made alive together with him [Christ], having
> forgiven us all our trespasses, by canceling the record of debt that
> stood against us with its legal demands. This he set aside, nailing it
> to the cross.

Those last words are the most crucial. "This—this record of debt
that stood against us—God set aside, nailing it to the cross." When
did that happen? Two thousand years ago. It did not happen inside of
us, and it did not happen with any help from us. God did it *for* us and
outside of us before we were ever born. This is the great objectivity of
our salvation.

Be sure you see this most wonderful and astonishing of all truths:
God took the record of all your sins that made you a debtor to wrath
(sins are offenses against God that bring down his wrath), and instead
of holding them up in front of your face and using them as the warrant to send you to hell, God put them in the palm of his Son's hand
and drove a spike through them into the cross. It is a bold and graphic
statement: He canceled the record of our debt . . . nailing it to the cross
(Col. 2:14).

Whose sins were nailed to the cross? Answer: *My* sins. And Noël's
sins. My wife's sins and my sins. The sins of all who despair of saving
themselves and who trust in Christ alone. Whose hands were nailed
to the cross? Jesus' were. There is a beautiful name for this. It's called a
substitution. God condemned *my* sin in *Christ's* flesh. "Sending his own
Son in the likeness of sinful flesh and for sin, he condemned sin in the
flesh" (Rom. 8:3). Husbands and wives cannot believe this too strongly.
It is essential to our fulfilling the design of marriage.

JUSTIFICATION GOES BEYOND FORGIVENESS

If we reach out further into the New Testament and draw in our understanding of justification from Romans, for example, we can say more. Justification goes beyond *forgiveness*. Not only are we forgiven because of Christ, but God also declares us *righteous* because of Christ. God requires two things of us: punishment for our sins and perfection in our lives. Our sins must be punished, and our lives must be righteous. But we cannot bear our own punishment (Ps. 49:7–8), and we cannot provide our own righteousness. "None is righteous; no, not one" (Rom. 3:10).

Therefore, God, out of his immeasurable love for us, provided his own Son to do both. Christ bears our punishment, and Christ performs our righteousness. And when we receive Christ (John 1:12), all of his punishment and all of his righteousness is counted as ours (Rom. 4:4–6; 5:1, 19; 8:1; 10:4; 2 Cor. 5:21; Phil. 3:8–9).

JUSTIFICATION BENT OUTWARD

This is the vertical reality that must be bent outward horizontally to our spouses if marriage is to display the covenant-making, covenant-keeping grace of God. We see this in Colossians 3:12–13:

> Put on then, as God's chosen ones, holy and beloved, compassionate hearts, kindness, humility, meekness, and patience, bearing with one another and, if one has a complaint against another, forgiving each other; as the Lord has forgiven you, so you also must forgive.

"As the Lord has forgiven you, so you also must forgive" your spouse. As the Lord "bears with" you, so you should bear with your spouse. The Lord "bears with" us every day as we fall short of his will. Indeed, the distance between what Christ expects of us and what we achieve is infinitely greater than the distance between what we expect of our spouse and what he or she achieves. Christ always forgives more and endures more than we do. *Forgive* as you have been forgiven. *Bear with* as he bears with you. This holds true whether you are married to a believer or an unbeliever. Let the measure of God's grace to you in the cross of Christ be the measure of your grace to your spouse.

And if you are married to a believer, you can add this: As the Lord counts you righteous in Christ, though you are not righteous in actual behavior and attitude, so count your spouse righteous in Christ, though he or she is not righteous. In other words, Colossians 3:12–13 says, take the vertical grace of forgiveness and justification and bend them out horizontally to your spouse. Marriage is meant to be a unique matrix for this display of God's grace. This is what marriage is for ultimately—the display of Christ's covenant-keeping grace.

THE NEED FOR GOSPEL-ROOTED WISDOM

Now at this point, hundreds of complex situations emerge that cry for deep spiritual wisdom rooted in these gospel truths and in long years of painful, faithful experience. In other words, there is no way I could apply this truth to everyone's particular needs in one chapter or one book. Besides this biblical truth, we need the Holy Spirit. We need prayer. We need to meditate on the Bible for ourselves. We need to read the insights of others. We need the counsel of wise friends who are seasoned with suffering. We need the church to support us when everything falls apart. So I have no illusions that I could say here all that needs to be said to help you.

LIVING VERTICALLY, THEN BENDING OUTWARD

It may help to close this chapter by giving several reasons why I am stressing covenant-love as forgiveness and as counting your spouse as righteous when he or she is not. Why the focus on the negative assumption that our spouse is a sinner in need of forgiveness? Don't I believe you should be delighted in your spouse? Yes, I do.

But both experience and the Bible push me there. To be sure, Jesus is married to his bride, the church, and clearly it is both possible and good to *please* the Lord (Col. 1:10). That is, Christ does find delight in his bride. And, on the other side, he certainly is infinitely worthy of our pleasure *in him*. This is the ideal to aim at in marriage: two people humbling themselves and seeking to change in godly ways that please their spouses and meet their physical and emotional needs—to please them in every good way. Yes. The relationship of Christ and the church includes all that.

But the reasons I stress living vertically from the grace of God and then bending out horizontally in forgiveness and justification toward your spouse are: 1) because there is going to be conflict based on sin and strangeness (and you won't be able even to agree with each other about what is simply strange about each other and what is sin); and 2) because the hard, rugged work of enduring and forgiving is what makes it possible for affections to flourish when they seem to have died; and 3) because God gets glory when two very different and very imperfect people forge a life of faithfulness in the furnace of affliction by relying on Christ.

I will pick it up here in the next chapter and tell you about a discovery that Noël and I made. We call it "the compost pile." For now, husbands and wives, drive into your own consciences these huge truths—greater than any problem in your marriage—that God "has forgiven us all our trespasses, by canceling the record of debt that stood against us with its legal demands. This he set aside, nailing it to the cross" (Col. 2:13–14). Believe this with all your heart, and bend it toward your spouse.

God gives you Christ as the foundation of your marriage. "Welcome one another, therefore, as Christ has welcomed you, for the glory of God" (Rom. 15:7). . . . Don't insist on your rights, don't blame each other, don't judge or condemn each other, don't find fault with each other, but accept each other as you are, and forgive each other every day from the bottom of your hearts.

DIETRICH BONHOEFFER,
Letters and Papers from Prison, 31–32

CHAPTER FOUR

FORGIVING AND FORBEARING

Put on then, as God's chosen ones, holy and beloved, compassionate hearts, kindness, humility, meekness, and patience, bearing with one another and, if one has a complaint against another, forgiving each other; as the Lord has forgiven you, so you also must forgive. And above all these put on love, which binds everything together in perfect harmony. And let the peace of Christ rule in your hearts, to which indeed you were called in one body. And be thankful. Let the word of Christ dwell in you richly, teaching and admonishing one another in all wisdom, singing psalms and hymns and spiritual songs, with thankfulness in your hearts to God. And whatever you do, in word or deed, do everything in the name of the Lord Jesus, giving thanks to God the Father through him. Wives, submit to your husbands, as is fitting in the Lord. Husbands, love your wives, and do not be harsh with them.

COLOSSIANS 3:12–19

Recall that there are at least three reasons my wife was right when she said, "You cannot say too often that marriage is a model of Christ and the church" (cf. Eph. 5:31–32). One was that saying this about marriage lifts it out of the sitcom sewer and elevates it into the bright, clear sky of God's glory where it is meant to be. Another was that saying this about marriage places it firmly on the basis of grace. By grace Christ *took* the church to be his bride in the first place, and by grace he *sustains* her. If marriage models that, it will be full of grace. This will be its ground and its glory. The third reason that we should stress often that marriage is a model of Christ and the church is that it profoundly shapes the way we understand headship and submission. We will deal with this in Chapters 6–8.

HUMAN MARRIAGE WILL VANISH

The first two chapters of this book were meant to support that first reason. I tried to show that marriage is the *doing* of God and the *display* of God—especially his grace. That is its glory—marriage is from him and through him and to him. This is the bright, clear sky of God's glory where marriage was meant to be.

Another way to see this is to recall that human marriage is temporary. To be sure, it points to something eternal, namely, Christ and the church. But when this age is over, it will vanish into the superior reality to which it points.

Jesus said in Matthew 22:30, "In the resurrection they neither marry nor are given in marriage, but are like angels in heaven." This is why my father, Bill Piper, will not be a bigamist in the resurrection. Both my mother and my stepmother have died. My father had a thirty-six-year marriage with my mother and, after her death, a twenty-five-year marriage with my stepmother. But in the resurrection, the shadow gives way to the reality. My father will not be married in heaven, either to my mother or to my stepmother. Marriage is a pointer toward the glory of Christ and the church. But in the resurrection the pointer vanishes into the perfection of that glory.

BENDING GRACE FROM VERTICAL TO HORIZONTAL

Then the point in Chapter 3 was that marriage is based on grace—the vertical experience of grace from Christ through his death on the cross, and then that very grace bent out horizontally from husband to wife and from wife to husband. Colossians 2:14 tells us how God provided a basis for the forgiveness of our sins: ". . . by canceling the record of debt that stood against us with its legal demands. This he set aside, nailing it to the cross." The record of debt that mounts up against us because of our sin God set aside by nailing it to the cross—and the point, of course, is not that nails and wood take away sin, but that the pierced hands and feet of the Son of God take away sin (see Isa. 53:5–6).

Having shown us the basis of God's forgiveness in the cross, Paul then says in Colossians 3:13, "As the Lord has forgiven you, so you also must forgive." In other words, take the forgiveness and justification that you have received vertically through the death of Christ and bend it out horizontally to others. Specifically, husbands to wives and wives to husbands.

WHY THE FOCUS ON FORGIVENESS?

I asked the question near the end of Chapter 3: Why this emphasis on forgiving and forbearing rather than, say, on romance and enjoying each other? I gave three answers: 1) because there is going to be conflict based on sin, we need to forgive *sin* and forbear *strangeness*, and sometimes you won't even agree on which is which; 2) because the hard, rugged work of forgiving and forbearing is what makes it possible for affections to flourish when they seem to have died; and 3) because God gets glory when two very different and very imperfect people forge a life of faithfulness in the furnace of affliction by relying on Christ.

TO SPARE YOU SEPARATION

So in this chapter, I want to deal more thoroughly with forbearing and forgiving. Let me say at the outset that I am aware—painfully aware—that there are sins that spouses commit against each other that can push forbearance and forgiveness across the line into the assisting of sin and may even warrant a redemptive separation—I choose the words carefully: a *redemptive separation*. I am thinking of things like assault, adultery, child abuse, drunken rage, addictive gambling or theft or lying that brings the family to ruin.

My aim in this chapter is not to talk about these—that will come later when we take up the topic of separation and divorce and remarriage. Here I am trying to describe a biblical pattern of forbearance and forgiveness that can keep you from reaching the point of separation, and maybe even bring some of you back from the brink—perhaps even restore some marriages that the world calls "divorced." And I pray this will also sow seeds in single people who may one day be married, so that you will build your marriage on this rock of grace.

THE FOUNDATION: THE PERSON AND WORK OF CHRIST

When Paul gets to Colossians 3:12, he has laid a massive foundation in the person and work of Christ on the cross. This is the foundation of marriage and all of life. The main battles in life and in marriage are battles to believe this person and this work. I mean *really* believe it—trust it, embrace it, cherish it, treasure it, bank on it, breathe it, shape your life by it. So when Paul gets to Colossians 3:12, he exhorts us with words that are explosive with emotion-awakening reality built on Christ and his saving work.

First there are three descriptions of you, the believer, that Paul uses to help you receive his exhortation. "Put on then, as God's *chosen ones, holy* and *beloved . . .*" He is about to tell us what kind of heart and attitude we should have—putting it on like a garment. But first he calls us *chosen, holy, loved.*

Chosen

We are God's elect. Before the foundation of the world, God chose us in Christ. You can hear how precious this is to Paul with his words from Romans 8:33: "Who shall bring any charge against God's elect?" The answer is that absolutely nobody can make a charge stick against God's elect. Paul wants us to feel the wonder of being elect as being invincibly loved. If you resist the truth of election, you resist being loved in the fullness and the sweetness of God's love.

Holy

Then he calls us *holy*—that is, set apart for God. He chose us for a purpose—to be his holy people. To come out of the world and not be common or unclean anymore. Ephesians 1:4: "He chose us in him before the foundation of the world, that we should be *holy*." First Peter 2:9: "You are a chosen race . . . a *holy* nation." This is first a position and a destiny before it is a pattern of behavior. That is why he is telling us the kind of behavior to "put on." He knows we are not there yet, practically. He is calling us to *become* holy in life because we *are* holy in Christ. Dress to fit who you are. Wear holiness.

Loved

Then he calls us *loved*. "God's *chosen ones, holy* and *beloved.*" If you are a believer in Christ, God, the maker of the universe, chose you, set you apart for himself, and loves you. He is for you and not against you. "God shows his love for us in that while we were still sinners, Christ died for us" (Rom. 5:8).

SEE AND SAVOR THESE THREE WONDERS

This is the beginning of how husbands and wives forbear and forgive. They are blown away by being *chosen, set apart*, and *loved* by God. Husbands, devote yourselves to seeing and savoring this. Wives, do the same. Get your life from this. Get your joy from this. Get your hope from this—that you are *chosen, set apart*, and *loved* by God. Plead with the Lord that this would be the heartbeat of your life and your marriage.

On this basis now—on the basis of this profound, new, God-centered identity as chosen, holy, and loved—we are told what to "put on." That is, we are told what kind of attitude and behavior fits with, and flows from, being chosen, set apart, and loved by God through Christ.

Paul shows us that there are three *inward* conditions that lead in turn to three *outward* demeanors. "Put on then, as God's chosen ones, holy and beloved, compassionate hearts, kindness, humility, meekness, and patience, bearing with one another and, if one has a complaint against another, forgiving each other." We will break it down into pairs: compassionate hearts and kindness, humility and meekness, patience and forbearance (and forgiveness).

From Bowels of Mercy to Kindness

"Put on then, as God's chosen ones, holy and beloved, *compassionate hearts, kindness*" (Col. 3:12). "Compassionate hearts" is a modern translation of the phrase "bowels of mercy." "Bowels of mercy" is the inward condition, and "kindness" is the outward demeanor. Be merciful in your inmost being, and then out of that good ground grows the fruit of kindness.

So husbands, sink your roots by faith into Christ through the gospel until you become a more merciful person. Wives, sink your roots by faith into Christ through the gospel until you become a more merciful person. And then treat each other out of this tender mercy with kindness. The battle is with our own unmerciful inner person. Fight that battle by faith, through the gospel, in prayer. Be stunned and broken and built up and made glad and merciful because you are chosen, holy, loved.

From Humility to Meekness

The next pair is "humility, meekness." Verse 12: "Put on then, as God's chosen ones, holy and beloved, compassionate hearts, kindness, *humility, meekness* . . ." Literally, "lowliness, meekness." Again "lowliness" is the inward condition, and "meekness" is the outward demeanor. People whose hearts are lowly, instead of proud, will act more meekly toward others. The meek count others above themselves and serve them. That happens when the heart is lowly, or humble.

So, husbands, sink your roots by faith into Christ through the gospel until you become more lowly and humble. Wives, sink your roots by faith into Christ through the gospel until you become more lowly and humble. The gospel of Christ's painful death on our behalf has a way of breaking our pride and our sense of rightful demands and our frustration at not getting our way. It works lowliness into our souls. Then we treat each other with meekness flowing out of that lowliness. The battle is with our own proud, self-centered inner person. Fight that battle by faith, through the gospel, in prayer. Be stunned and broken and built up and made glad and humble because you are chosen, holy, loved.

From Long-Suffering to Forbearance and Forgiveness

The next pair is not exactly a pair. It's an inner condition followed by forbearance *and* forgiveness. But forbearance and forgiveness are one. Neither can exist biblically without the other. Verse 12: "Put on then, as God's chosen ones, holy and beloved, compassionate hearts, kindness, humility, meekness, and *patience, bearing with* one another and, if one has a complaint against another, *forgiving* each other." So I am treating "patience" as the inner condition and forbearance/forgiveness as the outward demeanor or behavior.

The literal translation of patience is "long-suffering." That is, become the kind of person who does not have a short fuse but a long one. A very long one. Become a patient person, slow to anger, quick to listen, slow to speak (Jas. 1:19). These three inner conditions I have mentioned connect with each other and affect each other. "Bowels of mercy" and "lowliness" lead to being "long-suffering." If you are quick to anger, instead of being long-suffering, the root is probably lack of mercy and lack of lowliness. In other words, being chosen, holy, and loved has not broken your heart and brought you down from self-centeredness and pride.

So, husbands, sink your roots by faith into Christ through the gospel until your heart is formed by these inner conditions of compassion and lowliness and patience. Fight for inner change—making you more merciful and more lowly and, in that way, more long-suffering. In the same way, wives, sink your roots by faith into Christ through the gospel until you become more merciful and more lowly and more long-suffering.

Then treat each other with . . . what? This final pair is not exactly a pair. First, there was the pair of compassionate or merciful hearts leading to a demeanor of kindness. Then there was the pair of humility or lowliness leading to a demeanor of meekness. But now there is patience or long-suffering leading to what?

FORBEARING AND FORGIVING IN MARRIAGE

"Put on then, as God's chosen ones, holy and beloved . . . patience, *bearing with* one another and, if one has a complaint against another, *forgiving* each other" (Col. 3:12–13). The inner condition of patience is followed by two things, not one thing: first, "bearing with one another" and then, second, "if one has a complaint against another, forgiving each other." Forbearing and forgiving. What does this mean, and what does it look like in marriage?

First, a comment about the two words. *Forbear* or *bear with*: The word is literally *endure*—enduring each other. Jesus uses it in Luke 9:41: "O faithless and twisted generation, how long am I to *bear with* you?" Paul uses it again in 1 Corinthians 4:12: "When persecuted, we *endure*." That's the meaning here: Become long-suffering persons and endure each other. Forbear. "Love bears all things, believes all things, hopes all things, endures all things. Love never ends" (1 Cor. 13:7–8).

The other word is *forgive*. There are at least two words for *forgive* in the New Testament. This one used here (*charizomenoi*) means "freely or graciously give." The idea is that when we forgive, we do not exact a payment. We treat people better than they deserve. So in this sense, you forgive when someone has wronged you, and therefore they are in debt to you, and sheer justice says you have the right to exact some suffering from them in payment for the suffering they caused you. You not only don't demand the payment, but you "freely give" good for evil. That is the meaning of this word *forgive* (*charizomai*). Your ordinary disposition is forgiving—you do not return evil for evil, but you bless (Matt. 5:44; Luke 6:27; 1 Cor. 4:12; 1 Thess. 5:15).

"FOR BETTER OR FOR WORSE"

Now what I find so helpful here is that Paul recognizes that *both* forgiving *and* forbearing are crucial for life together—whether in church or marriage. Forgiveness says: I will not treat you badly because of your sins against me or your annoying habits. And forbearance acknowledges (usually to itself): Those sins against me and those annoying habits *really* bother me or hurt me! If there were nothing in the other person that really bothered us or hurt us, there would be no need for saying "endure one another."

When you marry a person, you don't know what they are going to be like in thirty years. Our forefathers did not craft wedding vows with their heads in the sand. Their eyes were wide-open to reality— "to have and to hold from this day forward, for better, *for worse*, for richer, *for poorer*, in *sickness* and in health, to love, honor, and cherish, 'til death do us part, and thereto I plight thee my troth [I pledge you my faithfulness]." You don't know what this person will be like in the future. It could be better than you ever dreamed, or worse. Our hope is based on this: We are chosen, holy, and loved. God is for us, and all things will work for the good of those who love him (Rom. 8:28; Ps. 23:6; 84:11).

THE COMPOST PILE

So what about the compost pile I mentioned at the end of the last chapter? Picture your marriage as a grassy field. You enter it at the beginning full of hope and joy. You look out into the future, and you see beautiful flowers and trees and rolling hills. And that beauty is what you see in each other. Your relationship is the field and the flowers and the rolling hills. But before long, you begin to step in cow pies. Some seasons of your marriage they may seem to be everywhere. Late at night they are especially prevalent. These are the sins and flaws and idiosyncrasies and weaknesses and annoying habits in you and in your spouse. You try to forgive them and endure them with grace.

But they have a way of dominating the relationship. It may not even be true, but sometimes it feels like that's all there is—cow pies. Noël and I have come to believe that the combination of forbearance and forgiveness leads to the creation of a compost pile. That's where you shovel the cow pies.

You both look at each other and simply admit that there are a lot of cow pies. But you say to each other: You know, there is more to this relationship than cow pies. And we are losing sight of that because we keep focusing on these cow pies. Let's throw them all in the compost pile. When we have to, we will go there and smell it and feel bad and deal with it the best we can. And then we are going to walk away from that pile and set our eyes on the rest of the field. We will pick some favorite paths and hills that we know are not strewn with cow pies. And we will be thankful for the part of the field that is sweet.

Our hands may be dirty. And our backs may ache from all the shoveling. But one thing we know: We will not pitch our tent by the compost pile. We will only go there when we must. This is a gift of grace that we will give each other again and again and again—because we are chosen and holy and loved.

POPPING THE BUBBLE OF NAIVETÉ

We are aware that some folks don't like this idea of a compost pile. They feel as if it is a concession to sin that compromises the possibilities of repentance and change. Believe me, we empathize with that. I hope the next chapter corrects any misunderstanding—as if we didn't believe in working hard at getting rid of cow-pie behavior entirely. We do believe in that. We believe in the pursuit of personal change and holiness. We believe in small-group efforts to work on each other's marriages. We believe in professional biblical counseling.

But we are forty years into this glorious and maddening thing called marriage, and we are not naive. These two redeemed sinners will go to our graves imperfect and annoying. We are very comforted that Paul does not say, "Endure one another for the first ten years of your marriage till you have all the problems solved and all the sins overcome, then enjoy the green pastures of the last forty years of your marriage without the need for enduring each other." Sorry to pop any bubbles out there. Well, actually, we're not sorry. We would rather pop the bubble of naiveté and give you a possible way to endure and enjoy. But we do hope you will read the next chapter to balance the point.

Thus the very hour of disillusionment with my brother becomes incomparably salutary, because it so thoroughly teaches me that neither of us can ever live by our own words and deeds, but only by that one Word and Deed which really binds us together—the forgiveness of sins in Jesus Christ. When the morning mists of dreams vanish, then dawns the bright day of Christian fellowship.

DIETRICH BONHOEFFER,
Life Together, 26–27

CHAPTER FIVE

PURSUING CONFORMITY TO CHRIST IN THE COVENANT

[Submit] to one another out of reverence for Christ. Wives, submit to your own husbands, as to the Lord. For the husband is the head of the wife even as Christ is the head of the church, his body, and is himself its Savior. Now as the church submits to Christ, so also wives should submit in everything to their husbands. Husbands, love your wives, as Christ loved the church and gave himself up for her, that he might sanctify her, having cleansed her by the washing of water with the word, so that he might present the church to himself in splendor, without spot or wrinkle or any such thing, that she might be holy and without blemish. In the same way husbands should love their wives as their own bodies. He who loves his wife loves himself. For no one ever hated his own flesh, but nourishes and cherishes it, just as Christ does the church, because we are members of his body. "Therefore a man shall leave his father and mother and hold fast to his wife, and the two shall become one flesh." This mystery is profound, and I am saying that it refers to Christ and the church. However, let each one of you love his wife as himself, and let the wife see that she respects her husband.

EPHESIANS 5:21–33

Y ou cannot say too often that marriage is a model of Christ and the church. That's what Noël said. One of the reasons she is right is that this makes clear that marriage is based on grace. Christ pursues his bride by grace, obtains her for his own by grace, sustains her by grace, and will perfect her for himself by grace. We deserve none of this. We deserve judgment. It is all by grace.

BETTER THAN WE DESERVE

In the previous two chapters, we have emphasized that this grace empowers husbands and wives to keep their covenant by means of forgiveness and forbearance. That emphasis is at the heart of what grace is: treating people better than they deserve. This is one of the central pieces of Christian ethics:

> "Love your enemies, do good to those who hate you, bless those who curse you, pray for those who abuse you. To one who strikes you on the cheek, offer the other also, and from one who takes away your cloak do not withhold your tunic either . . . love your enemies, and do good, and lend, expecting nothing in return, and your reward will be great, and you will be sons of the Most High, for he is kind to the ungrateful and the evil. Be merciful, even as your Father is merciful." (Luke 6:27–29, 35–36)

Those commands do not cease to be demands of Jesus when we get married. If we are to return good for evil in general, how much more in marriage.

GRACE IS ALSO THE POWER TO CHANGE

That's what we have emphasized so far in saying that marriage is based on God's grace toward us. But now I want to emphasize another truth about grace: It not only gives power to endure being sinned against, it also gives power to stop sinning.

In all our emphasis on forgiving and forbearing, you might get the impression that none of our sinful traits or our annoying idiosyncrasies ever change—or ever should change. So all we can do is forgive and forbear. But what I want to try to show from Scripture now is that God gives grace not only to forgive and to forbear, but also to change, so that less forgiving and forbearing is needed. That too is a gift of grace. Grace is not just the power to return good for evil; it is also the power to do less evil—even power to be less bothersome. Grace makes you want to change for the glory of Christ and for the joy of your spouse. And grace is the power to do it.

Even as I write this, I tremble that it will be misused by a frustrated spouse. I fear that you will take it as mainly applying to your spouse and not to you. "Finally Piper is going to stop telling me to endure her, and start telling her to change." May I plead with you to take what I say here first for *yourself* and not first for your spouse. Focus first on *your* need to change, not on hers or his. It may be that your spouse is sinning against you far more than you are against him or her. But you will not give an account for that to the Lord Jesus. You *will* give an account for your responses to it. That is the great battle. Will *you* change? Yes, your spouse should change. No doubt about it. But I promise you, it will not bear the fruit you want, if that is your main focus.

THE ROUNDABOUT GOSPEL WAY

You might think we have arrived at this point of talking about personal change in a roundabout way. Why put the emphasis on forgiveness and forbearance first? This emphasis came first because it's the essential rock-solid foundation for change. In other words, rugged covenant-keeping commitment based on grace gives security and hope so the call for change can be heard without feeling like a threat. Only when a wife or husband feels that the other is totally committed—even if he or she doesn't change—can the call for change feel like grace rather than an ultimatum.

So in this chapter I am emphasizing that marriage *should* not be and, God willing, *need* not be static—no change, just endurance. Even that is better than divorce in God's eyes and has a glory of its own. But it is not the best picture of Christ and the church. Yes, our endurance in a troubled marriage tells a truth about Christ and the church—it is a troubled relationship because of our sin, not his. But there are other truths about Christ and the church that need to be displayed. It is not an honor to Christ if we think we should display those truths by being unwilling to change our sinful and annoying behaviors.

BEYOND FORGIVENESS AND FORBEARANCE

That brings us to the key text for this chapter, Ephesians 5:25–27. These verses relate directly to the theme of this chapter, the pursuit of conformity to Christ in the covenant of marriage. Listen to how these verses take us beyond forgiveness and forbearance in the way husbands are to love their wives:

> Husbands, love your wives, as Christ loved the church and gave himself up for her, that he might sanctify her, having cleansed her by the washing of water with the word, so that he might present the church to himself in splendor, without spot or wrinkle or any such thing, that she might be holy and without blemish.

In Christ's relationship to the church, he is clearly seeking the transformation of his bride into something morally and spiritually beautiful. And he is seeking it at the cost of his life. Let's think for a moment about the implications of this passage on how a husband thinks and acts with a view to changing his wife. We will come to the wife's desire to change her husband shortly.

The first implication is that the husband, who loves like Christ, bears a unique responsibility for the moral and spiritual growth of his wife—which means that over time, God willing, there will be change.

TREADING ON DANGEROUS GROUND

I realize that at this point—no matter how I come at this—I am treading on dangerous ground. I could be playing right into the hands of a selfish, small-minded, controlling husband who has no sense of the difference between enriching differences between him and his wife and moral and spiritual weaknesses or defects that should be changed. Such a man may distort what I am saying into a mandate to control every facet of his wife's behavior, and the criteria of what he seeks to change will be his own selfish desires cloaked in spiritual language.

This is no laughing matter. I have had to deal with husbands who were pathological in their understanding of a wife's submission. One woman told me, as we were sorting through their dysfunctional relationship, that her husband demands that she get permission for going to the bathroom. I'm not making that up. Certain kinds of minds seem unable to bring many truths to bear on a relationship at one time. They are small, narrow, sick minds. They oversimplify. They distort. They ruin. I pray that nothing I say will be used by them to justify their sin.

An honest look at Ephesians 5:25–27 will help us steer a loving, wise, mature course through this minefield. Consider three observations:

1. The Husband Is Not Christ

The husband is *like* Christ, which means he is *not* Christ. Verse 23: "The husband is the head of the wife even *as* Christ is the head of the church." The word *as* does not mean that the husband is like Christ in every way. The husband is finite in strength, not omnipotent like Christ. The husband is finite and fallible in wisdom, not all-wise like Christ. The husband is sinful, not perfect like Christ. Therefore, we husbands dare not assume we are infallible. We sometimes err in what we would like to see changed in our wives. That's the first observation.

2. Conformity to Christ, Not to the Husband

The aim of the godly husband's desire for change in his wife is conformity to Christ, not conformity to himself. Notice the key words in verses 26–27. Verse 26: "that he [Christ] might *sanctify* her." Verse 27: "that he [Christ] might present the church to himself in *splendor*." Verse 27 again: "that she might be *holy*." These words—*sanctify, splendor, holy*—imply that our desires for our wives are measured by God's standard of holiness, not our standard of personal preferences.

3. Dying for the Wife

The third observation is the most important: What Paul draws attention to most amazingly is that the way Christ pursues his bride's transformation is by dying for her. Verses 25–26: "Husbands, love your wives, as Christ loved the church and *gave himself up for her*, that he might sanctify her." This is the most radical thing that could ever be said to a husband about the way he leads his wife into conformity to Christ in the covenant of marriage. Husbands, are we pursuing her conformity to Christ by lording it over her or by dying for her? When we lead her or even, if necessary, confront her, are we self-exalting or self-denying? Is there contempt or compassion?

If a husband is loving and wise like Christ in all these ways, his desire for his wife's change will feel, to a humble wife, like she is being served, not humiliated. Christ clearly desires for his bride to grow in holiness. But he *died* to bring it about. So we husbands should govern our desire for our wife's change by the self-denying death of Christ. May God give us the humility and the courage to measure our methods by the sufferings of Christ. (See Titus 2:14; Rev. 19:7.)

WIVES CHANGING HUSBANDS

Now we turn to the wife's desire for her husband's change. This chapter is not about what headship and submission are. But to make clear what I am saying about how we help each other change, I have to touch on what headship and submission are *not*. I have already said that a husband's headship is not identical to Christ's headship. It is *like* it. Similarly, therefore, the wife's submission to the husband is not identical to her submission to Christ. It is *like* it.

When Ephesians 5:22 says, "Wives, submit to your own husbands, *as* to the Lord," the word *as* does not mean that Christ and the husband are the same. Christ is supreme; the husband is not. Her allegiance is first to Christ, not first to her husband. The analogy only works if the woman submits to Christ absolutely, not to the husband absolutely. Then she will be in a position to submit to the husband without committing treason or idolatry.

What this implies is that a wife will see the need for change in her husband. He is not perfect like Christ is. He is flawed. Therefore, the wife may and should seek the transformation of her husband, even while respecting him as her head—her leader, protector, and provider. There are several other reasons I say this.

THE ANALOGY OF PRAYER

One reason is the function of prayer in the relationship between Christ and his church. A wife relates to her husband the way the church should relate to Christ. The church prays to Christ—or to God the Father through Christ. When the church prays to her Husband, she asks him to do things a certain way. If we are sick, we ask him for healing. If we are hungry, we ask for our daily bread. If we are lost, we ask for direction. And so on. Since we believe in the absolute sovereignty of Christ to govern all things, this means that we look at the present situation that he has ordained, and we ask him to change it.

I am only drawing out an analogy here, not an exact comparison. The church never confronts Jesus with his imperfection. He has no imperfections. But we do seek from him changes in the situation he has brought about. That is what petitionary prayer is. So wives, on this analogy, will ask their husbands to change some ways he is doing things.

ALL HUSBANDS NEED CHANGE

But the main reason we can say that wives may and should seek their husbands' transformation is that husbands are only *similar* to Christ in the relationship with their wives. We are not Christ. And one of the main differences is that our character and habits need to change, and Christ's don't. We are *like* Christ in the relationship, but we are not Christ. Unlike Christ, we are sinful and finite and fallible. We need to change. That is a clear and universal New Testament teaching. All men and women need to change.

WIVES ARE LOVING SISTERS IN CHRIST

Another factor to take into account is that wives are not only wives, but in Christ they are also loving sisters. There is a unique way for a submissive wife to be a caring sister toward her imperfect brother-husband. She will, for example, from time to time, follow Galatians 6:1 in his case: "If anyone is caught in any transgression, you who are spiritual should restore him in a spirit of gentleness." She will do that for him.

And not only Galatians 6:1, but other passages as well. For example, both of them—spiritual husband and spiritual wife—will obey Matthew 18:15 as necessary, and will do so with the unique demeanor called for by headship and submission: "If your brother sins against you, go and tell him his fault, between you and him alone."

THE DANGER OF NAGGING

All of this has to be balanced by the danger of nagging. It is a sad thing when a woman longs for her man to step up and take responsibility in leading the family spiritually and he won't do it. We will say more about that in the chapters to come. But the word *nag* exists in English to warn us that there is such a thing as *excessive* exhortation.

The apostle Peter warns against this with strong words in 1 Peter 3:1. He says, "Wives, be subject to your own husbands, so that even if some do not obey the word, they may be won *without a word* by the conduct of their wives." This is talking mainly about an unbelieving husband, but the principle applies more widely.

I don't think 1 Peter 3:1 means a wife cannot talk to her husband about her faith. But surely it does mean that there is a kind of speaking that is counterproductive. "Without a word" means, don't badger him. Don't nag him. Be as wise as a serpent and as innocent as a dove (Matt. 10:16). Discern whether any word would be heard. Mainly, Peter says, try to win your husband by your "respectful and pure conduct" (1 Pet. 3:2).

BOTH SEEK CHANGE BY SACRIFICE

Which brings us back to our main text in Ephesians 5. Paul said to husbands, "Husbands, love your wives, as Christ loved the church and gave himself up for her, that he might sanctify her" (verses 25–26). It isn't only wives who seek to win their spouses by their behavior. This is the primary means by which Christ won the church. He died for her. So wives win their husbands mainly by their lives of sacrificial love, and husbands win their wives mainly by lives of sacrificial love.

FORGIVING AND FORBEARING WERE MORE THAN WE THOUGHT

Which means, when you stop and think about it, that everything I wrote about forgiving and forbearing in the previous chapters turns out to be not merely a means of enduring what will not change, but also a means of changing by means of sacrificial, loving endurance. Few things have a greater transforming impact on a husband or a wife than the long-suffering, forgiving sacrifices of love in the spouse. There is a place for confrontation. There is a place for pursuing conformity to Christ in the covenant of marriage. Life is not all forgiveness and forbearance. Real change can happen. Real change ought to happen. Christ died to make it happen. And he calls us, husbands and wives, to love like that.

Now when the husband is called "the head of the wife," and it goes on to say "as Christ is the head of the church" (Eph. 5:23), something of the divine splendor is reflected in our earthly relationships, and this reflection we should recognize and honor. The dignity that is here ascribed to the man lies, not in any capacities or qualities of his work but in the office conferred on him by his marriage. The wife should see her husband clothed in this dignity. But for him it is supreme responsibility.

DIETRICH BONHOEFFER,
Letters and Papers from Prison, 30

LIONHEARTED AND LAMBLIKE—
THE CHRISTIAN HUSBAND AS HEAD:
FOUNDATIONS OF HEADSHIP

[Submit] to one another out of reverence for Christ. Wives, submit to your own husbands, as to the Lord. For the husband is the head of the wife even as Christ is the head of the church, his body, and is himself its Savior. Now as the church submits to Christ, so also wives should submit in everything to their husbands. Husbands, love your wives, as Christ loved the church and gave himself up for her, that he might sanctify her, having cleansed her by the washing of water with the word, so that he might present the church to himself in splendor, without spot or wrinkle or any such thing, that she might be holy and without blemish. In the same way husbands should love their wives as their own bodies. He who loves his wife loves himself. For no one ever hated his own flesh, but nourishes and cherishes it, just as Christ does the church, because we are members of his body. "Therefore a man shall leave his father and mother and hold fast to his wife, and the two shall become one flesh." This mystery is profound, and I am saying that it refers to Christ and the church. However, let each one of you love his wife as himself, and let the wife see that she respects her husband.

EPHESIANS 5:21–33

The reason I am using the title "Lionhearted and Lamblike" to refer to the Christian husband as head of his wife is because the husband is called to lead like Jesus who is the Lion of Judah (Rev. 5:5) and the Lamb of God (Rev. 5:6)—he was lionhearted and lamblike, strong and meek, tough and tender, aggressive and responsive, bold and broken-hearted. He sets the pattern for manhood.

In this chapter and the one following, we will focus on what it means for a married man to be the head of his wife and of his home. We focus on this for two reasons. One is that the Bible says in Ephesians 5:23, "The husband is the head of the wife as Christ is the head of the church." We need to know what the Bible means by this statement so that we can exult in it and obey.

The other reason is that few things are more broken in our day than manhood and headship in relation to women and families. The price of this brokenness is enormous and touches almost every facet of life. So for the sake of faithful biblical exposition and exultation, and for the sake of recovering biblical manhood and Christ-exalting family structures, we will devote two chapters to this important issue of headship.

FIRST THINGS FIRST

One of the emphases so far in this book has been that staying married is not mainly about staying in love, but about keeping covenant. We did eventually come around to saying that precisely by this unwavering covenant-keeping the possibility of being profoundly in love in forty years is much greater than if you think the task of marriage is first staying in love. Keeping first things first makes second things better. Staying in love isn't the first task of marriage. It is a happy overflow of covenant-keeping for Christ's sake.

We have spent most of our effort in these chapters pondering the foundations of covenant-keeping in the way Christ keeps covenant with us. We have looked at marriage as a showcase of covenant-keeping grace and as a combination of forgiveness and forbearance. And in the previous chapter we took up the question, *Can you help each other change?* And if so, how do you do that graciously?

Until now we have spent little time on the distinct roles of husband and wife—headship and submission. This was intentional. Foundations in the gospel are needed before these things can shine with the beauty they really have. There is nothing ugly or undesirable in these distinctions of headship and submission when they're seen in the light of the gospel of grace.

So now the question presses on us: What is headship? And what is submission? The plan is to deal with headship in this and the next chapter and then deal separately with submission in Chapter 8.

This chapter will be largely *foundation* for headship, and the next chapter will be largely *application*. What is the basis of headship, and what does it look like in practice?

THE MYSTERY REVEALED

Ephesians 5 is starting to feel like an old friend. Let's move into the text at verse 31. It's a quote from Genesis 2:24: "Therefore a man shall leave his father and mother and hold fast to his wife, and the two shall become one flesh." In the next verse (v. 32), Paul looks back on this quote and says, "This mystery is profound, and I am saying that it refers to Christ and the church."

Now why is the coming together of a man and woman to form one flesh in marriage called a *mystery*? *Mystery* in the New Testament does not mean something too complex or deep or obscure or distant for humans to understand. It refers to a hidden purpose of God that is now revealed for our understanding and enjoyment. Paul explains what the mystery is in verse 32. The marriage union is a mystery, he says, because its deepest meaning has been concealed by God during the Old Testament history but is now being openly revealed by the apostle, namely, that marriage is an image of Christ and the church. Verse 32: "I am saying that it refers to Christ and the church."

So marriage is like a metaphor or an image or a picture or a parable or a model that stands for something more than a man and a woman becoming one flesh. It stands for the relationship between Christ and the church. That's the deepest meaning of marriage. It's meant to be a living drama of the covenant-keeping love between Christ and the church.

THE PARALLEL BETWEEN ONE BODY AND ONE FLESH

You can see how this is confirmed in verses 28–30. They describe the parallel between Christ and the church being *one body* and the husband and wife being *one flesh*. Verses 28–29: "In the same way husbands should love their wives as their own bodies. He who loves his wife loves himself. For no one ever hated his own flesh, but nourishes and cherishes it." In other words, the one-flesh union between man and wife means that in a sense they are now one body so that the care a husband has for his wife he, in that very act, has for himself. They are one. What he does for her he does for himself.

Then Paul compares this to Christ's care for the church. Verses 29–30: "No one ever hated his own flesh, but nourishes and cherishes it, just as Christ does the church, *because we are members of his body.*" Be sure to see the parallel: Christ nourishes and cherishes the church because we are members (that is, arms and legs and hands and feet) of his body. And husbands nourish and cherish their wives "as their own bodies." No one ever hated *his own flesh.* Wives are our own flesh as the church is Christ's own body. Just as the husband is *one flesh* with his wife, so Christ is *one body* with the church. When the husband cherishes and nourishes his wife, he cherishes and nourishes himself; and when Christ cherishes and nourishes the church, he cherishes and nourishes himself.

All of this underlines what Paul calls a "profound mystery"—that marriage, in its deepest meaning, is a copy of Christ and the church. If you want to understand God's meaning for marriage, you have to grasp that we are dealing with a copy of an original, a metaphor of a greater reality, a parable, and a greater truth. The *original,* the *reality,* the *truth* refer to God's marriage to his people, or now in the New Testament we see it as Christ's marriage to the church. And the *copy,* the *metaphor,* the *parable* refer to human marriage between a husband and a wife. In one of the best books on marriage I have read, Geoffrey Bromiley says, "As God made man in His own image, so He made earthly marriage in the image of His own eternal marriage with His people."[1] I think that is exactly right. And it is one of the most profound things you can say about human life.

CHRIST/CHURCH, HEAD/BODY, HUSBAND/WIFE

One of the things to learn from this mystery is that the roles of husband and wife in marriage are distinct. Consider the way Ephesians 5:22–25

---

[1]Geoffrey Bromiley, *God and Marriage* (Grand Rapids, MI: Eerdmans, 1980), 43.

unpacks the role of husband and the role of wife in the mystery of marriage as a copy of Christ and the church.

> Wives, submit to your own husbands, as to the Lord. For the husband is the head of the wife even as Christ is the head of the church, his body, and is himself its Savior. Now as the church submits to Christ, so also wives should submit in everything to their husbands. Husbands, love your wives, as Christ loved the church and gave himself up for her.

Husbands are compared to Christ; wives are compared to the church. Husbands are compared to the head; wives are compared to the body. Husbands are commanded to love as Christ loved; wives are commanded to submit as the church is to submit to Christ.

It is astonishing how many people do not see this when they deal with this passage. Or, seeing it, they neglect it. I have in mind those who would be called *egalitarians*—the ones who reject the idea that men are called to be leaders in the home. They put all the emphasis on verse 21 and the teaching of mutual submission. All agree that verse 21 is overflow from verse 18 where Paul commands us to be filled with the Spirit. Verses 18–21 read like this:

> Be filled with the Spirit, addressing one another in psalms and hymns and spiritual songs, singing and making melody to the Lord with your heart, giving thanks always and for everything to God the Father in the name of our Lord Jesus Christ, *submitting to one another* out of reverence for Christ.

Submitting to one another is seen as an expression of being filled with the Holy Spirit. Husbands and wives who are filled with the Holy Spirit serve one another. They humble themselves and get down low to lift the other up. They find ways to submit their immediate preferences for comfort to the need of the other. Amen to that! May it happen more and more. I have no desire to minimize the mutuality of submission and servanthood.

MUTUAL SUBMISSION AND UNIQUE ROLES

But the problem is that egalitarians seem to stop with mutual submission, as if that were all one needed to say about roles in marriage, or as if that is all that the text has to say. And when they stop there, most people today are left with great ambiguity and great confusion about the proper roles of husband and wife. Once you clarify for people that a husband and a wife should be mutually humble and mutually ready to serve each other and mutually eager to meet each other's needs and build each other up—once you have said all that, there remains a great uncertainty as to what, if anything, distinguishes the role of husband and wife. Is it only the biological gift of childbearing that distinguishes the roles? Or is there something more pervasive?

What is so astonishing is that egalitarians don't embrace what every ordinary reader can see in Ephesians 5. After declaring that there is mutual submission in verse 21, Paul devotes twelve verses to unfolding the *difference* in the way a husband and wife should serve each other. You don't need to deny mutual submission to affirm the importance of the unique role of the husband as head and the unique calling of the wife to submit to that headship.

The simplest way to see this is to remember that Jesus himself bound himself with a towel and got down on the floor and washed his disciples' feet (the bridegroom serving the bride), but not for one minute did any of the apostles in that room doubt who the leader was in that moment. In other words, mutuality of submission and servanthood do not cancel out the reality of leadership and headship. Servanthood does not nullify leadership; it defines it. Jesus does not cease to be the Lion of Judah when he becomes the lamblike servant of the church.

After calling attention to the mutuality of submission or servanthood in verse 21, Paul devotes the whole passage through verse 33 to making *distinctions* between the role of the husband and the role of the wife—between the loving headship of a husband who takes his cues from Christ and the willing submission of a wife who takes her cues from how the church is to follow Christ. What we need to hear from this text today is not just a call to mutual submission that leaves young men groping for what it means to be a husband and young women groping for what it means to be a wife. What we need to hear is what headship and submission mean. What are the positive, practical implications of being called *head* that give man his distinct role in marriage?

It is not enough to say, "Serve one another." That is true of Christ and his church—they serve each other. But they do *not* serve each other in all the same ways. Christ is Christ. We are the church. To confuse the distinctions would be doctrinally and spiritually devastating. So also the man is the Christ-portraying husband, and the woman is the church-portraying wife. And to confuse these God-intended distinctions, or to abandon them, results in more disillusionment and more divorce and more devastation.

NOT ARBITRARY OR REVERSIBLE

One of the things that is crystal-clear in Ephesians 5 is that the roles of husband and wife in marriage are not arbitrarily assigned, and they are not reversible any more than the role of Christ and the church are reversible. The roles of husband and wife are rooted in the distinctive roles of Christ and his church. The revelation of this mystery is the recovery of the original intention of covenant marriage in the Garden of Eden.

You can see this most clearly when you ponder what sin did to headship and submission and how Paul's teaching here in Ephesians 5 is so perfectly suited to remedy that corruption. When sin entered the world, it ruined the harmony of marriage not because it brought headship and submission into existence, but because it twisted man's humble, loving headship toward hostile domination in some men and lazy indifference in others. And it twisted woman's intelligent, willing, happy, creative, articulate submission toward manipulative obsequiousness in some women and brazen insubordination in others. Sin didn't create headship and submission; it ruined them and distorted them and made them ugly and destructive.

RECOVERING ROLES FROM THE RAVAGES OF SIN

Now if this is true, then the redemption we anticipate with the coming of Christ is not the dismantling of the original, created order of loving headship and willing submission, but a recovery of it from the ravages of sin. And that's exactly what we find in Ephesians 5:21–33. Wives, let your fallen submission be redeemed by modeling it after God's intention for the church! Husbands, let your fallen headship be redeemed by modeling it after God's intention for Christ!

Therefore, headship is not a *right* to control or to abuse or to neglect. (Christ's sacrifice is the pattern.) Rather, it's the *responsibility* to love like Christ in leading and protecting and providing for our wives and families. Submission is not slavish or coerced or cowering. That's not the way Christ wants the church to respond to his leadership and protection and provision. He wants the submission of the church to be free and willing and glad and refining and strengthening.

In other words, Ephesians 5:21–33 does two things: It guards against the abuses of headship by telling husbands to love like Jesus, and it guards against the debasing of submission by telling wives to respond the way Christ calls the church to submit to him.

TOWARD SOME DEFINITIONS

So let me close this chapter with brief definitions of headship and submission and then turn in the next chapter to practical application of what this headship in particular looks like.

Headship is the divine calling of a husband to take primary responsibility for Christlike, servant leadership, protection, and provision in the home.

Submission is the divine calling of a wife to honor and affirm her husband's leadership and help carry it through according to her gifts.[2]

A good deal is at stake here. I hope you take it seriously, whether you are single or married, old or young. Not just the fabric of society hangs on this, but the revelation of the covenant-keeping Christ and his covenant-keeping church.

---

[2]See the next chapter for the biblical basis of the words *leadership*, *protection*, and *provision*.

As the head, it is he who is responsible for his wife, for their marriage, and for their home. On him falls the care and protection of the family; he represents it to the outside world; he is its mainstay and comfort; he is the master of the house, who exhorts, punishes, helps, and comforts, and stands for it before God. It is a good thing, for it is a divine ordinance when the wife honors the husband for his office's sake, and when the husband properly performs the duties of his office.

DIETRICH BONHOEFFER,
Letters and Papers from Prison, 30

LIONHEARTED AND LAMBLIKE—
THE CHRISTIAN HUSBAND AS HEAD:
WHAT DOES IT MEAN TO LEAD?

[Submit] to one another out of reverence for Christ. Wives, submit to your own husbands, as to the Lord. For the husband is the head of the wife even as Christ is the head of the church, his body, and is himself its Savior. Now as the church submits to Christ, so also wives should submit in everything to their husbands. Husbands, love your wives, as Christ loved the church and gave himself up for her, that he might sanctify her, having cleansed her by the washing of water with the word, so that he might present the church to himself in splendor, without spot or wrinkle or any such thing, that she might be holy and without blemish. In the same way husbands should love their wives as their own bodies. He who loves his wife loves himself. For no one ever hated his own flesh, but nourishes and cherishes it, just as Christ does the church, because we are members of his body. "Therefore a man shall leave his father and mother and hold fast to his wife, and the two shall become one flesh." This mystery is profound, and I am saying that it refers to Christ and the church. However, let each one of you love his wife as himself, and let the wife see that she respects her husband.

EPHESIANS 5:21–33

Jesus sets the pattern of manhood as the Lion of Judah and the Lamb of God. He was in his strongest and weakest moments a leader, provider, and protector. But it may not yet be clear to some that the concept of headship involves leadership as its main meaning. In this regard, the key verse on headship is Ephesians 5:23: "The husband is the *head* of the wife even as Christ is the *head* of the church, his body, and is himself its Savior." So the husband is to take his unique cues in marriage from Christ in his relationship to his church. I take that to mean that the husband bears a unique responsibility for leadership in the marriage.

FACETS OF LEADERSHIP

I suggested at the end of the previous chapter that a biblical definition of headship would be: *Headship is the divine calling of a husband to take primary responsibility for Christlike, servant leadership, protection, and provision in the home.* The more I have thought about those three facets of headship—leadership, protection, and provision—the more it seems to me that they really resolve into one thing with two expressions. Leadership is the one thing, and protection and provision are the two expressions. In other words, a husband's leadership expresses itself in taking the lead in seeing to it that the family is protected and provided for. So protection and provision are not separate from leadership. They are the two fundamental areas where the husband is called upon to bear primary responsibility.

So what we need to do is see the support for this in the Scripture and then some application or illustration of what it means. Consider a few arguments from Ephesians for why the word *head* in verse 23 involves a unique responsibility of leadership.

BEING HEAD INVOLVES LEADERSHIP

First, the term *head* is used for leaders in the Old Testament. For example, Judges 11:11: "So Jephthah went with the elders of Gilead, and the people made him head and leader over them [*eis kephalēn kai eis archēgon*]." (See also Judg. 10:18; 11:8–9; 2 Sam. 22:44; Ps. 18:43; Isa. 7:8.)

Second, Ephesians 1:21–23 says that Christ is "above every name that is named . . . and [God] has put all things under his feet and has made him the *head* over all things to the church, which is his body." The focus in this text is on Christ's rule and authority when he is called head of the church. So the emphasis falls on his leadership over the church.

Third, in Ephesians 5:25 Paul says, "Husbands, love your wives, as Christ loved the church and gave himself up for her." While the stress here falls on Christ's sacrifice for his bride and so tells the husband to love like this, we must not miss the inescapable truth that Christ took an absolutely decisive action here. He was not responding to the church. The church did not plan its salvation and sanctification. Christ did. This is leadership of the most exalted kind. But it is servant leadership. Christ is taking the lead to save his bride, and he is doing it by suffering and dying for her.

We see leadership in Christ's sacrifice not only in the fact that he planned it and took the initiative, but also in the fact that he died to give an example to us. Jesus said, "If anyone would come after me, let him deny himself and take up his cross and follow me" (Matt. 16:24). In other words, "I have taken the lead in suffering for love's sake; now you take up your cross and follow me." This is why leadership is not mainly a right and privilege, but a burden and a responsibility.

Finally, in view of these three reasons why headship involves leadership, the fourth argument is that the concept of submission, when related to headship, implies that headship is leadership. Paul says in verses 22–23, "Wives, submit to your own husbands, as to the Lord. For the husband is the head of the wife." When the ground of the wife's submission is expressed as the headship of the husband, it is clear that headship involves the kind of leadership that a woman can affirm and honor.

The definition of *submission* that we will unfold in Chapter 8 is: "*Submission* is the divine calling of a wife to honor and affirm her husband's leadership and help carry it through according to her gifts." The point here is simply that when submission is correlated with headship, it implies that headship involves leadership. The wife honors and affirms her husband's leadership and helps carry it through according to her gifts.

So from these four observations—and there are more from other parts of the Bible that we could look at—I conclude that *headship is the divine calling of a husband to take primary responsibility for Christlike, servant leadership, protection, and provision in the home.*

Leading as Protector

Now where in this text do we see the idea that this leadership takes special responsibility for protection and provision in the family? First, consider protection. In verses 25–27 Paul shows the husband how to love his wife—that is, how to exercise the kind of servant leadership that Christ did:

> Husbands, love your wives, as Christ loved the church and *gave himself up for her*, that he might sanctify her, having cleansed her by the washing of water with the word, so that he might present the church to himself in splendor, without spot or wrinkle or any such thing, that she might be holy and without blemish.

In the words "gave himself up for her," we hear the saving sacrifice of Jesus Christ. When Christ gave himself for us, he took our place. He "bore our sins" (1 Pet. 2:24) and became a curse for us (Gal. 3:13) and died for us (Rom. 5:8); and because of all this we are reconciled to God and saved from—protected from!—his wrath, as Romans 5:10 says: "If while we were enemies we were reconciled to God by the death of his Son, much more, now that we are reconciled, shall we be saved by his life."

If there ever was an example of leadership that took the initiative to save and protect his bride, this is it. So when Paul calls a husband to be the head of his wife by loving like Christ when he leads, whatever else he means, he means: Protect her at all costs.

Leading as Provider

What about provision? I am contending that *headship is the divine calling of a husband to take primary responsibility for Christlike, servant leadership, protection, and provision in the home.* Are there evidences in this text that a husband's leadership should take primary responsibility for the provision of his wife and family? If anything, this is even more explicit. Consider verses 28–29: "In the same way husbands should love their wives as their own bodies. He who loves his wife loves himself. For no one ever hated his own flesh, but *nourishes and cherishes* it, just as Christ does the church."

The words *nourish* and *cherish* are significant. The word *nourish* (*ektrephei*) is most often used in the Bible for raising children and providing them with what they need, but the part of that meaning that applies here is not that the husband is a parent but that he is a caring provider. It is used more in the sense of Genesis 45:11, where Joseph says to his brothers, "I will *provide* [*ekthrepsō*] for you, for there are yet five years of famine to come." So the point is at least that the husband who leads like Christ takes the initiative to see to it that the needs of his wife and children are met. He provides for them.

Similarly, the other word in Ephesians 5:29 points in the same direction but even more tenderly. The husband "nourishes and *cherishes* [*thalpei*] it [his body, his wife], just as Christ does the church." This word for cherishing is used by Paul one other time, namely, to refer to his tender love for the church in Thessalonica. He compares himself to a mother caring for her infant. In 1 Thessalonians 2:7 Paul says, "We were gentle among you, like a nursing mother *taking care* of her own children." The point was not at all to belittle the church; the point was to emphasize his tender care and that he would do anything he could for them the way a mother does for her child.

So I conclude that there is good reason from Ephesians 5—not to mention Genesis 1–3 and elsewhere—to lift up the divine calling of the husband as bearing a *primary responsibility for Christlike, servant leadership, protection, and provision in the home.*

LIFE HANGS ON PROTECTION AND PROVISION

Now notice something about protection and provision. The reason they stand out is that they are so basic. Without protection and provision, life itself is threatened. So the reason these two rise to the surface so quickly is that if a husband fails in his leadership here, there may not be any other place to exercise it. The life of the family hangs on protection and provision. Life itself must be protected and nourished, or it ceases to exist.

But there is another reason these two stand out. Protection and provision both have a physical *and* a spiritual meaning. There is physical food that needs to be provided, and there is spiritual food that needs to be provided. Husbands need to protect against physical threats to the life of the family and spiritual threats to the life of the family. So when you think it through, virtually everything a husband is called upon to do in his leadership is summed up in one of these four ways: 1) physical provision (like food and shelter), 2) spiritual provision (like the word of God and spiritual guidance, instruction, and encouragement), 3) physical protection (as from intruders or natural disasters or disease), and 4) spiritual protection (like prayer and warnings and keeping certain influences out of the home). Provision: physical and spiritual. Protection: physical and spiritual.

ENCOURAGEMENT AND CAUTION

Before I give some examples, let me give a word of encouragement and caution. The encouragement is to men. If this sounds new and overwhelming, be encouraged that Christ does not call you to do what he won't empower you to do. My father loved to quote to us as a family Philippians 4:13, "I can do all things through him who strengthens me." Husbands are called to do some very hard things. Leadership is not easy. That's part of what being a Christian means: "Take up your cross and follow me." But with every command comes a promise. "Fear not, for I am with you; be not dismayed, for I am your God; I will strengthen you, I will help you, I will uphold you with my righteous right hand" (Isa. 41:10). So be encouraged. Leadership is hard. But you're a man. If your father never taught you how to lead, your heavenly Father will.

The caution is to women. You cannot demand that your husband take leadership. For several reasons: 1) *Demanding* is contradictory to the very thing for which you long. It is out of character. If you become the demander, he's not the leader. 2) Demanding will be counterproductive because if he had any impulse to try harder, your demanding will take the heart out of it, because it won't feel like leading anymore; it will feel like acquiescence to your demand. 3) It has to come from inside him brought about by the word of God and the Spirit of God.

So, instead of demanding, 1) pray earnestly for him that God would awaken his true manhood. 2) When you are neither tired nor angry, ask him for a time when the two of you alone can talk about your heart's desires. When you express your longings, do it without sounding any ultimatums and with a sense of hope grounded in God, not man. Express appreciation and honor for any ways that he is leading.

EXAMPLES AND EXPLANATIONS

That's the encouragement and the caution. Now some examples and explanations. These must be brief and provocative rather than an attempt to answer all possible questions. Consider what leadership is in each of the four spheres mentioned earlier.

1. Leadership in Spiritual Provision

To provide spiritual food for the family, you must know spiritual food. This means that a man must go hard after God. You can only lead spiritually if you are growing in your own knowledge of God and love for God. If you are feeding your soul with the word of God, you will be drawn to feed your wife and your children.

Gather your wife and children for family devotions every day—call it whatever you want: family prayers, family worship, family Bible time, devotions, etc. Take the initiative to gather them. If you don't know what to do, ask some brothers what they do. Or ask your wife what she would like to do. You don't have to be a loner here. Remember, headship takes *primary* responsibility, not *sole* responsibility. The wife, we pray, is always supporting and helping. And she regularly has gifts that the husband doesn't. What women rightly long for is spiritual and moral initiative from a man, not spiritual and moral domination.

And remember, there is no necessary connection between being an effective leader and being more intellectual or more competent than your wife. Leadership does not assume it is superior. It assumes it should take initiative. See that the family prays, and reads the Bible, and goes to church, and discusses spiritual and moral issues, and learns to use the means of grace, and grows in knowledge, and watches your example in all these things.

2. Leadership in Physical Provision

The husband bears the *primary* responsibility to put bread on the table. Again the word *primary* is important. Both husbands and wives work.

In all of history this has been the case—both the man and the woman work. But their normal spheres of work are man: breadwinner; wife: domestic manager, designer, nurturer.

That never has meant there are not seasons in life when a wife cannot work outside the home or that the husband cannot share the domestic burdens. But it does mean that a man compromises his own soul and sends the wrong message to his wife and children when he does not position himself as the one who lays down his life to put bread on the table. He may be disabled and unable to do what his heart longs to do. He may be temporarily in school while she supports the family. But in any case his heart—and, if possible, his body—is moving toward the use of his mind and his hands to provide physically for his wife and children.

3. Leadership in Spiritual Protection

The spiritual dangers that beset the family today are innumerable and subtle. We need valiant warriors like never before. Not with spears and shields, but with biblical discernment and courage. First, husbands, pray for your family every day, "Lead them not into temptation but deliver them from evil." Fight for them in prayer against the devil and the world and the flesh. Pray the prayers of the Bible for them. Don't grow weary. God hears and answers prayer for our wives and children.

Set standards for your wife and children. Work them through with your wife. Remember, the path of leadership here is *primary* responsibility, not sole responsibility. Wives are eager to help here, but they are frustrated when we don't take any initiative and they are left to try to determine and enforce the standards alone.

Take the initiative in thinking through what will be allowed on TV. What movies you and the children will go to. What music will be listened to. And how low your daughter's necklines will be. Dad has a crucial role in defining the modesty of his daughter's clothing. Yes, mom is the key player here in helping a young woman learn the meaning of modesty and beauty. But dad's role is indispensable both in celebrating what they look like and telling them when the way they dress means what they don't think it means. Dads know exactly what

I mean. What you need here is courage. Don't be afraid here. This is your daughter, and she must hear from you what she is saying to men with her clothes.

One other example of leadership in spiritual protection: Paul says in Ephesians 4:26–27, "Do not let the sun go down on your anger, and give no opportunity to the devil." In other words, one wide-open door to the devil in your house is unresolved anger as you go to bed—anger in the children and in the marriage. Leadership means we must take the lead in reconciliation.

I don't mean that wives should never say they are sorry. But in the relation between Christ and his church, who took the initiative to make all things new? Who left the comfort and security of his throne of justice to put mercy to work at Calvary? Who came back to Peter first after three denials? Who has returned to you again and again forgiving you and offering his fellowship afresh? Jesus, the Leader, the great initiative-taker.

So, husbands, your headship means: Go a*head*. Take the lead. It does not matter if it is her fault. That didn't stop Christ. Who will break the icy silence first? Who will choke out the words, "I'm sorry, I want it to be better"? Or "Can we talk? I'd like things to be better." She might beat you to it. Sometimes that's okay. But woe to you if you think that since it's her fault, she's obliged to say the first reconciling word. Headship is not easy. It is the hardest, most humbling work in the world. Protect your family. Strive, as much as it lies within you, to make peace before the sun goes down.

4. Leadership in Physical Protection

This is too obvious to need illustration—I wish. If there is a sound downstairs during the night and it might be a burglar, you don't say to her, "This is an egalitarian marriage, so it's your turn to go check it out. I went last time." And I mean that—even if your wife has a black belt in karate. After you've tried to deter him, she may finish off the burglar with one good kick to the solar plexus. But you'd better be unconscious on the floor, or you're no man. That's written on your soul, brother, by God Almighty. Big or little, strong or weak, night or day, you go up against the enemy first. Woe to the husbands—and woe to the nation—that send their women to fight their battles.

THE HUSBAND NO WIFE REGRETS

When Adam and Eve sinned in the garden and God came to call them to account, it didn't matter that Eve had sinned first. God said, "Adam, where are you?" (Gen. 3:9). That's God's word to the family today: Adam, husband, father, where are you? If something is not working right at the Piper house and Jesus comes knocking on the door, he may have an issue with my wife, but the first thing he's going to say when she opens the door is, "Is the man of the house home?" That's the way it happened in the first marriage. That's the way it will happen in our marriage.

When a man joyfully bears the primary God-given responsibility for Christlike, servant leadership and provision and protection in the home—for the spiritual well-being of the family, for the discipline and education of the children, for the stewardship of money, for the holding of a steady job, for the healing of discord—I have never met a wife who is sorry she married such a man. Because when God designs a thing (like marriage), he designs it for his glory and our good.

God establishes a rule of life by which you can live together in wedlock: "Wives, be subject to your husbands, as is fitting in the Lord. Husbands, love your wives" (Col. 3:18, 19). With your marriage you are founding a home. That needs a rule of life, and this rule of life is so important that God establishes it himself, because without it everything would be out of joint. You may order your home as you like, except in one thing: the wife is to be subject to her husband and the husband is to love his wife.

DIETRICH BONHOEFFER,
Letters and Papers from Prison, 28

CHAPTER EIGHT

THE BEAUTIFUL FAITH OF FEARLESS SUBMISSION

Likewise, wives, be subject to your own husbands, so that even if some do not obey the word, they may be won without a word by the conduct of their wives, when they see your respectful and pure conduct. Do not let your adorning be external—the braiding of hair and the putting on of gold jewelry, or the clothing you wear—but let your adorning be the hidden person of the heart with the imperishable beauty of a gentle and quiet spirit, which in God's sight is very precious. For this is how the holy women who hoped in God used to adorn themselves, by submitting to their own husbands, as Sarah obeyed Abraham, calling him lord. And you are her children, if you do good and do not fear anything that is frightening.

1 PETER 3:1–6

Having devoted two chapters to a husband's role as head in the marriage, we turn now to the wife's counterpart—submission. I am very eager that men and women, single and married, old and young, hear this as a call to something strong and noble and beautiful and dignified and worthy of a woman's highest spiritual and moral efforts.

To set the stage for that impact, notice two phrases in 1 Peter 3:1: "Likewise, wives, be subject to your own husbands." Notice the word *own* in "your *own* husbands." That means that there is a uniquely fitting submission to your own husband that is not fitting in relation to other men. You are not called to submit to all men the way you do to your husband. Then notice the phrase at the beginning: "Likewise, wives."

This means that the call for a wife's submission is part of a larger call for submission from all Christians in different ways.

SUBMISSION FOR ALL CHRISTIANS

In 1 Peter 2:13–17, Peter admonishes us *all* to be subject, "for the Lord's sake," to every human institution, whether it be to the emperor as supreme or to governors appointed by him. In other words, keep the speed limits, pay your taxes, and be respectful toward policemen and senators.

Then in 2:18–25 Peter addresses the household servants (*oiketai*) in the church and admonishes them to be submissive to their masters with all respect, both to the kind and to the overbearing.

Then in 3:1–6 Peter instructs the wives to be submissive to their husbands, including the husbands who are unbelieving. This is the part we will focus on in this chapter.

Then in verse 7 he instructs husbands to live considerately with their wives as fellow heirs of the grace of life.

Finally, in 3:8–12, Peter tells the whole church to have unity and sympathy and love and tenderheartedness and humility toward one another, and not to return evil for evil. In other words, submit to each other and serve each other. So, as we saw in Ephesians 5, submission is a wider Christian virtue for all of us to pursue, and it has its unique and fitting expressions in various relationships. In this chapter we are focusing on the relationship of a wife to her husband. What does submission look like there?

THE ROOTS OF WOMANHOOD

Before I describe what submission isn't and what it is, let's gaze briefly at the powerful portrait of womanhood that Peter paints for us in these words. What we see is the deep strong roots of womanhood underneath the fruit of submission. It's the roots that make submission the strong and beautiful thing that it is.

Let's start with verse 5: "This is how the holy women who hoped in God used to adorn themselves, by submitting to their own husbands." The deepest root of Christian womanhood mentioned in this text is hope in God. "Holy women who *hoped in God* . . ." A Christian woman does not put her hope in her husband, or in getting a husband. She does not put her hope in her looks or her intelligence or her creativity. She puts her hope in the promises of God. She is described in Proverbs 31:25: "Strength and dignity are her clothing, and she laughs at the time to come." She laughs at everything the future could bring because she hopes in God.

She looks away from the troubles and miseries and obstacles of life that seem to make the future bleak, and she focuses her attention on the sovereign power and love of God who rules in heaven and does on earth whatever he pleases (Ps. 115:3). She knows her Bible, and she knows her theology of the sovereignty of God, and she knows his promise that he will be with her and will help her and strengthen her no matter what. This is the deep, unshakable root of Christian womanhood. And Peter makes it explicit in verse 5. He is not talking about just any women. He is talking about women with unshakable biblical roots in the sovereign goodness of God—holy women who hope in God.

FEARLESSNESS

The next thing to see about Christian womanhood, after hope in God, is the fearlessness that it produces in these women. So verse 5 says that the holy women of old hoped in God. And then verse 6 gives Sarah, Abraham's wife, as an example and then refers to all other Christian women as her daughters. Verse 6: "And you are her children, if you do good and *do not fear anything that is frightening*."

So this portrait of Christian womanhood is marked first by hope in God and then by what grows out of that hope, namely, fearlessness. She does not fear the future; she laughs at the future. The presence of hope in the invincible sovereignty of God drives out fear. Or to say it more carefully and realistically, the daughters of Sarah fight the anxiety that rises in their hearts. They wage war on fear, and they defeat it with hope in the promises of God.

Mature Christian women know that following Christ will mean suffering (2 Tim. 3:12). But they believe promises like 1 Peter 3:14, "But even if you should suffer for righteousness' sake, you will be blessed. Have no fear of them, nor be troubled," and 1 Peter 4:19, "Therefore let those who suffer according to God's will entrust their souls to a faithful Creator while doing good." That is what Christian women do: They entrust their souls to a faithful Creator. They hope in God. And they triumph over fear.

INTERNAL ADORNMENT

This leads to a third feature of Peter's portrait of womanhood, a focus on internal adornment rather than external. First Peter 3:5 begins, "This is how the holy women who hoped in God used to adorn themselves." This adornment refers back to what is described in verses 3–4:

> Do not let your adorning be external—the braiding of hair and the putting on of gold jewelry, or the clothing you wear—but let your adorning be the hidden person of the heart with the imperishable beauty of a gentle and quiet spirit, which in God's sight is very precious.

We know this does not mean that all jewelry and all hair styling are excluded. Then all clothing would be excluded as well, because it says, "Do not let your adorning be external . . . the clothing you wear." What he means is: Don't focus your main attention and effort on how you look on the outside; focus it on the beauty that is inside. Exert more effort and be more concerned with inner beauty than outer beauty.

And he is specific in verse 4. When a woman puts her hope in God and not her husband and not in her looks, and when she overcomes fear by the promises of God, this will have an effect on her heart: It will give her an inner tranquillity. That's what Peter means in verse 4 by "the imperishable beauty of a *gentle and quiet spirit*, which in God's sight is very precious."

A UNIQUE KIND OF SUBMISSIVENESS

That leaves one more feature of this portrait of womanhood to see. First, there was hope in God. That leads then to fearlessness in the face of whatever the future may bring. Then that leads to an inner tranquillity and meekness. And, finally, that spirit expresses itself in a unique kind of submissiveness to her husband. Verse 1: "Likewise, wives, *be subject to your own husbands.*" Verse 5: "This is how the holy women who hoped in God used to adorn themselves, by *submitting to their own husbands.*"

That is a brief look at the portrait of the kind of woman Peter has in mind when he calls a woman to be submissive to her husband. Unshakable hope in God. Courage and fearlessness in the face of the future. Quiet tranquillity of soul. Humble submission to her husband's leadership.

THE SADNESS OF SCORNED BEAUTY

It is a great sadness that in our society—even in the church—the different and complementary roles of biblical headship for the husband and biblical submission for the wife are despised or simply passed over. Some people just write them off as sub-Christian cultural leftovers from the first century. Others distort and misuse them—I mentioned earlier that I actually sat in my office once with a husband who believed that submission meant his wife should not go from one room to the other in the house without asking his permission. That kind of pathological distortion makes it easier for people to dispense with texts like these in the Bible.

But the truth of headship and submission is really here and really beautiful. When you see it lived out with the mark of Christ's majesty on it—the mutuality of servanthood without canceling the reality of headship and submission—it is a wonderful and deeply satisfying drama. So let's ponder from this text first what submission is not, and then what it is.

WHAT SUBMISSION IS NOT

Here are six things it is *not*, based on 1 Peter 3:1–6.

1. Submission does not mean agreeing with everything your husband says. You can see that in verse 1: She is a Christian, and he is not. He has one set of ideas about ultimate reality. She has another. Peter calls her to be submissive while assuming she will not submit to his view of the most important thing in the world—God. So submission can't mean submitting to agree with all her husband thinks.

2. *Submission does not mean leaving your brain or your will at the wedding altar.* It is not the inability or the unwillingness to think for yourself. Here is a woman who heard the gospel of Jesus Christ. She thought about it. She assessed the truth claims of Jesus. She perceived in her heart the beauty and worth of Christ and his work, and she chose him. Her husband heard it also. Otherwise Peter probably wouldn't say he "disobeyed the word." He has heard the gospel, and he has thought about it. And he has not chosen Christ. She thought for herself, and she acted. And Peter does not tell her to retreat from that commitment.

3. *Submission does not mean avoiding every effort to change a husband.* The whole point of this text is to tell a wife how to win her husband. Verse 1 says, "Be subject to your own husbands, so that even if some do not obey the word, they may be won without a word by the conduct of their wives." If you didn't care about the Bible, you might say, "Submission has to mean taking a husband the way he is and not trying to change him." But if you believe what the Bible says, you conclude that submission, paradoxically, is sometimes a strategy for changing him.

4. *Submission does not mean putting the will of the husband before the will of Christ.* The text clearly teaches that the wife is a follower of Jesus before and above being a follower of her husband. Submission to Jesus relativizes submission to husbands—and governments and employers and parents. When Sarah called Abraham "lord" in verse 6, it was *lord* with a lowercase *l.* Peter is referring to Genesis 18:12: "Sarah laughed to herself, saying, 'After I am worn out, and *my lord* is old, shall I have pleasure?'"

What is astonishing about this reference is that Peter passed over the most amazing instance of Sarah's submission, namely, when Abraham wanted her to say in Egypt that she was his sister. At the risk of her life and sexual abuse, she obeyed. Peter did *not* choose to illustrate his point with this instance. I suspect he did not like holding it up as a model. Abraham was not loving her as he ought. Instead Peter illustrates his point about Sarah's submission by referring to a statement where she called Abraham *lord* incidentally. It was a mere aside. It was not intended for Abraham to hear; she was talking to herself. It gives a simple glimpse into her heart. She honors him when no one is listening. The word is like "sir" or "m'lord." And the obedience she rendered is qualified obedience because her supreme allegiance is to the Lord with a capital *L*.

5. *Submission does not mean that a wife gets her personal, spiritual strength primarily through her husband.* A good husband should indeed strengthen and build up and sustain his wife. He should be a source of strength. But what this text shows is that when a husband's spiritual leadership is lacking, a Christian wife is not bereft of strength. Submission does not mean she is dependent on him to supply her strength of faith and virtue and character. The text, in fact, assumes just the opposite. She is summoned to develop depth and strength and character not *from* her husband but *for* her husband. Verse 5 says that her hope is in God and in the power of God that one day her husband will join her in the faith.

6. *Finally, submission does not mean that a wife is to act out of fear.* Verse 6 says, "You are her [Sarah's] children, if you do good and do not fear anything that is frightening." In other words, submission is free, not coerced. The Christian woman is a free woman. When she submits to her husband—whether he is a believer or unbeliever—she does it in freedom, not out of fear.

WHAT SUBMISSION IS

If that's what submission is not, then what is it? At the end of Chapter 6, based on Ephesians 5, I suggested that *submission is the divine calling of a wife to honor and affirm her husband's leadership and help carry it through according to her gifts.* That's what we see here as well. It's the disposition to follow a husband's authority, and an inclination to yield to his leadership. It is an attitude that says, "I delight for you to take the initiative in our family. I am glad when you take responsibility for things and lead with love. I don't flourish in the relationship when you are passive and I have to make sure the family works."

But submission does not follow a husband into sin. What then does submission say in such a situation? What does submission say to a husband who is leading a wife into sin? It says, "It grieves me when you venture into sinful acts and want to take me with you. You know I can't do that. I have no desire to resist you. On the contrary, I flourish most when I can respond joyfully to your lead; but I can't follow you into sin, as much as I love to honor your leadership in our marriage. Christ is my King."

The reason I say that submission is a *disposition* and an *inclination* to follow a husband's lead is because there will be times in a Christian marriage when the most submissive wife, with good reason, will hesitate at a husband's decision. It may look unwise to her. Suppose it's Noël and I. I am about to decide something for the family that looks foolish to her. At that moment Noël could express her submission like this: "Johnny, I know you've thought a lot about this, and I love it when you take the initiative to plan for us and take the responsibility like this, but I really don't have peace about this decision, and I think we need to talk about it some more. Could we? Maybe tonight sometime?"

The reason that is a kind of biblical submission is 1) because husbands, unlike Christ, are fallible and ought to admit it; 2) because husbands ought to want their wives to be excited about the family decisions, since Christ wants the church to be excited about following his decisions and not just follow begrudgingly; 3) because the way Noël expressed her misgivings communicated clearly that she endorses my leadership and affirms me in my role as head; and 4) because she has made it clear to me from the beginning of our marriage that if, when we have done all the talking we should, we still disagree, she will defer to her husband's decision.

GOD'S WAY IS GOOD FOR US

So I end this chapter with the reminder that marriage is not mainly about staying in love. It's about covenant-keeping. And the main reason it is about covenant-keeping is that God designed the relationship between a husband and his wife to represent the relationship between Christ and the church. This is the deepest meaning of marriage. And that is why ultimately the roles of headship and submission are so important. If our marriages are going to tell the truth about Christ and his church, we cannot be indifferent to the meaning of headship and submission. And let it not go unsaid that God's purpose for the church—and for the Christian wife who represents it—is her everlasting, holy joy. Christ died for her to bring that about.

Thus it begins; the cross is not a terrible end to an otherwise God-fearing and happy life, but it meets us at the beginning of our communion with Christ. When Christ calls a man, he bids him come and die. . . . "Rejoice and be exceeding glad: for great is your reward in heaven." There shall the poor be seen in the halls of joy. With his own hand God wipes away the tears from the eyes of those who had mourned upon the earth. He feeds the hungry at his Banquet. There stand the scarred bodies of the martyrs, now glorified and clothed in the white robes of eternal righteousness instead of the rags of sin and repentance. The echoes of this joy reach the little flock below as it stands beneath the cross, and they hear Jesus saying: "Blessed are ye!"

DIETRICH BONHOEFFER,
The Cost of Discipleship, 99, 128

CHAPTER NINE

SINGLE IN CHRIST:
A NAME BETTER THAN SONS
AND DAUGHTERS

Thus says the LORD: "Keep justice, and do righteousness, for soon my salvation will come, and my deliverance be revealed. Blessed is the man who does this, and the son of man who holds it fast, who keeps the Sabbath, not profaning it, and keeps his hand from doing any evil." Let not the foreigner who has joined himself to the LORD say, "The LORD will surely separate me from his people"; and let not the eunuch say, "Behold, I am a dry tree." For thus says the LORD: "To the eunuchs who keep my Sabbaths, who choose the things that please me and hold fast my covenant, I will give in my house and within my walls a monument and a name better than sons and daughters; I will give them an everlasting name that shall not be cut off. "And the foreigners who join themselves to the LORD, to minister to him, to love the name of the LORD, and to be his servants, everyone who keeps the Sabbath and does not profane it, and holds fast my covenant— these I will bring to my holy mountain, and make them joyful in my house of prayer; their burnt offerings and their sacrifices will be accepted on my altar; for my house shall be called a house of prayer for all peoples."

ISAIAH 56:1–7

Why is there a chapter on singleness in a book on marriage? First, it's here to keep married people from idolizing marriage. It's here to keep us from elevating the marriage state higher than we should. Second, it's here because some singles will read this book and need to see the fuller picture of how singleness and marriage relate to each other and to God's larger purposes. Third, it's here so that married and single people will be motivated to be part of the one primary family that is more important than all other families. Man-wife-children families are temporary blessings for this age. In the age to come, they will not exist (Matt. 22:23–30). But the church will exist as family forever. This has profound implications for how singles and married people think about each other and relate to each other.

I will start and end this chapter with my main point and, in the middle, cover a wide terrain of Scripture to support it. My main point is that God promises those who remain single in Christ blessings that are better than the blessings of marriage and children, and he calls you to display, by the Christ-exalting devotion of your singleness, the truths about Christ and his kingdom that shine more clearly through singleness than through marriage and child-rearing. What truths shine more brightly through singleness?

1) The truth that the family of God grows not by propagation through sexual intercourse, but by regeneration through faith in Christ;[1]

2) The truth that relationships in Christ are more permanent, and more precious, than relationships in families (and, of course, it is wonderful when relationships in families *are* also relationships in Christ; but we know that is often not the case);

3) The truth that marriage is temporary and finally gives way to the relationship to which it was pointing all along: Christ and the church—the way a picture is no longer needed when you see face-to-face;

4) The truth that faithfulness to Christ defines the value of life; all other relationships get their final significance from this. No family relationship is ultimate; relationship to Christ is.

To say the main point more briefly: God promises spectacular blessings to those of you who remain single in Christ, and he gives you an extraordinary calling for your life. To be single in Christ is, therefore,

---

[1] I borrow here from the expression of Barry Danylak, *A Biblical Theology of Singleness* (Cambridge, UK: Grove Books Limited, 2007), 13–16, which is an overflow from Danylak's doctoral studies at Cambridge University. This chapter draws heavily on his approach to the issue of singleness in the Bible.

not a falling short of God's best, but a path of Christ-exalting, covenant-keeping obedience that many are called to walk.

BETTER BLESSINGS THAN SONS AND DAUGHTERS

Now let's step back and look at the Scriptures, starting with Isaiah 56:4–5:

> Thus says the LORD: "To the eunuchs [those who cannot procreate but turn their lives into a unique service instead of marriage] who keep my Sabbaths, who choose the things that please me and hold fast my covenant, I will give in my house and within my walls a monument[2] and a name better than sons and daughters; I will give them an everlasting name that shall not be cut off."

God promises to bless obedient eunuchs with blessings that are better than sons and daughters. In other words, by implication, God promises those of you who remain single in Christ blessings that are better than the blessings of marriage and children.

COVENANT PEOPLE AND PROCREATION

But to see this more clearly we need to get the bigger picture. In the created order that God put in place before sin was in the world, and in the covenantal order that God put in place with the Jewish people from Abraham to the coming of Christ, God was primarily building his covenant people through procreation. God was focusing his covenant-keeping faithfulness mainly on an ethnic people. Therefore, being married and having offspring was of paramount importance for one's name and one's inheritance and for the preservation of God's covenant people.

So in Genesis 1:28, the first thing God says to Adam and Eve is "Be

---

[2]The literal translation of the Hebrew is "within my walls a *hand* and a name better than sons and daughters." For the sense behind the word *hand* (translated as *monument*), compare 2 Samuel 18:18, where Absalom says, "'I have no son to keep my name in remembrance.' He called the pillar after his own name, and it is called Absalom's *hand* to this day" (literal rendering, usually rendered *monument*). Absalom had built this memorial by himself and for himself (v. 18). So he had extended his memory into the future by his own *hand*. Perhaps then the idea of a hand is that the good that comes to us in the future, or the memorial that keeps us in remembrance in the future, is our ongoing *effect* as though our hand were still active.

fruitful and multiply and fill the earth." And in the account of Genesis 2:18, when woman was not yet created, God said, "It is not good that the man should be alone; I will make him a helper fit for him."

And when Abraham was chosen as the father of God's people, God took him out and showed him the stars and said, "So shall your offspring be" (Gen. 15:5). When Abraham could not have a son because of Sarah's barrenness, Abraham said, "Oh that Ishmael might live before you!" But God answered, "No, . . . Sarah your wife shall bear you a son" (Gen. 17:18–19). In other words, the physical offspring mattered. And it would come in God's way.

God reaffirms the same to Isaac in Genesis 26:3: "I will be with you and will bless you, for to you and to *your offspring* I will give all these lands, and I will establish the oath that I swore to Abraham your father." Again physical "offspring" are crucial for the covenant.

OFFSPRING FOR THE SAKE OF THE NAME

These offspring are crucial not only for the preservation of the covenant but also because a person's name would end if he had no children. So Saul asks David to swear that he will not cut off his offspring *for the sake of his name.* "Swear to me therefore by the LORD that you will not cut off my offspring after me, and that you will not destroy my name out of my father's house" (1 Sam. 24:21).

Remember the whole elaborate system of Levirate marriage—that is, the marriage of a man to his deceased brother's wife so that the name of the deceased brother would not be lost. The rule was that the first son born would bear the dead brother's name. Deuteronomy 25:6: "The first son whom she bears shall succeed to the name of his dead brother, that his name may not be blotted out of Israel." That's an amazing provision for the perpetuation of the name through physical seed.

The most famous instance of this is when Boaz agreed to marry Ruth to preserve the name of Elimelech, her father-in-law, and Mahlon, her husband. Boaz said, "Ruth the Moabite, the widow of Mahlon, I have bought to be my wife, to perpetuate the name of the dead in his inheritance, that the name of the dead may not be cut off from among his brothers and from the gate of his native place. You are witnesses this day" (Ruth 4:10).

So you can see how crucial marriage and offspring and the preservation of a name and an inheritance were in Israel. No wonder that Jephthah's daughter asked for two months, not to bewail her impending death, but to mourn that she was never married. Judges 11:37–38: "She said to her father, 'Let this thing be done for me: leave me alone two months, that I may go up and down on the mountains and weep for my virginity, I and my companions.' So he said, 'Go.'"

ISAIAH'S PROPHECY: "HE SHALL SEE HIS OFFSPRING"

All of this is the background that makes Isaiah 56:4–5 shine like the sun to eunuchs and others without marriage and children: "Thus says the LORD: 'To the eunuchs who keep my Sabbaths, who choose the things that please me and hold fast my covenant, I will give in my house and within my walls a monument and a name better than sons and daughters; I will give them an everlasting name that shall not be cut off.'" So without marriage and without children, these covenant-keeping eunuchs get a name and a memorial better than sons and daughters.

Where did this amazing promise come from? What's the basis of it, and what is it pointing toward? The key is Isaiah 53. This is the great prophecy of the sufferings of Christ who "was wounded for our transgressions [and] . . . crushed for our iniquities" (v. 5). In Isaiah 53, we sometimes overlook these words in verse 10: "It was the will of the LORD to crush him; he has put him to grief; when his soul makes an offering for guilt, *he shall see his offspring*; he shall prolong his days; the will of the LORD shall prosper in his hand."

"*He shall see his offspring.*" Here is a great prophecy: When the Messiah dies as "an offering for guilt" and rises again to "prolong his days" forever, he will by that great saving act produce many children: He will "see his offspring." In other words, the new people of God formed by the Messiah will *not* be formed by physical procreation but by the atoning death of Christ.

Which is why the next chapter (Isaiah 54) begins, "Sing, O barren one, who did not bear; break forth into singing and cry aloud, you who have not been in labor! For the children of the desolate one will be more than the children of her who is married" (Isa. 54:1). And this is also why Isaiah 56:5 says that unmarried covenant-keeping people will have "a monument and a name better than sons and daughters . . . [and] an everlasting name that shall not be cut off." In the true people of God formed by Jesus Christ, monuments, names, offspring, and inheritances do not arise through marriage and procreation.

JESUS, PAUL, AND PETER

So when we come now to the New Testament, Jesus makes clear that his people—the true people of God—will be produced not by physical procreation but by spiritual regeneration. So he says to Nicodemus, "Truly, truly, I say to you, unless one is born again he cannot see the kingdom of God" (John 3:3).

And Paul says in Galatians 3 to Jews and Gentiles alike, "Know then that it is those *of faith* who are the sons of Abraham. . . . [I]n Christ Jesus you are all sons of God, *through faith*" (vv. 7, 26). In other words, it is not physical descent from Abraham that makes you part of the covenant people of God but faith in Christ.

And Peter says that our inheritance comes not through marriage and offspring but through the work of Christ and the new birth: "According to his great mercy, he has caused us to be *born again* to a living hope through the resurrection of Jesus Christ from the dead, to an inheritance that is imperishable, undefiled, and unfading, kept in heaven for you" (1 Peter 1:3–4).

So Jesus, Paul, and Peter all say: Children are born into God's family and receive their inheritance not by marriage and procreation but by faith and regeneration. Which means that single people in Christ have zero disadvantage in bearing children for God and may, in some ways, have a great advantage.

The apostle Paul was single in Christ, and he said of his converts, "Though you have countless guides in Christ, you do not have many fathers. For I became your father in Christ Jesus through the gospel"

(1 Cor. 4:15). Paul was a great father and never married. And does he not speak beautifully for single women in Christ in 1 Thessalonians 2:7 when he writes, "We were gentle among you, like a nursing mother taking care of her own children"? So it will be said of many single women in Christ, "She was a great mother and never married."

A RADICAL RELATIONAL REORDERING

Take heed here lest you minimize what I am saying and do not hear how radical it really is. I am not sentimentalizing singleness to make the unmarried feel better. I am declaring the temporary and secondary nature of marriage and family over against the eternal and primary nature of the church. Marriage and family are temporary for this age; the church is forever. I am declaring the radical biblical truth that being in a human family is no sign of eternal blessing, but being in God's family means being eternally blessed. Relationships based on family are temporary. Relationships based on union with Christ are eternal. Marriage is a temporary institution, but what it stands for lasts forever. "In the resurrection," Jesus said, "they neither marry nor are given in marriage, but are like angels in heaven" (Matt. 22:30).

And when his own mother and brothers asked to see him, Jesus said, "'Who is my mother, and who are my brothers?' And stretching out his hand toward his disciples, he said, 'Here are my mother and my brothers!'" (Matt. 12:48–49). Jesus is turning everything around. Yes, he loved his mother and his brothers. But those are all natural and temporary relationships. He did not come into the world to focus on that. He came into the world to call out a people for his name from all the families of the earth into a new family where single people in Christ are full-fledged family members on a par with all others, bearing fruit for God and becoming mothers and fathers of the eternal kind.

"Blessed is the womb that bore you, and the breasts at which you nursed!" a woman cried out to Jesus. And he turned and said, "Blessed rather are those who hear the word of God and keep it!" (Luke 11:27–28). The mother of God is the obedient Christian—married or single! Take a deep breath and reorder your world.

"Truly, I say to you, there is no one who has left house or brothers or sisters or mother or father or children or lands, for my sake and for the gospel," Jesus said, "who will not receive a hundredfold now in this time, houses and brothers and sisters and mothers and children and lands, with persecutions, and in the age to come eternal life" (Mark 10:29–30). Single person, married person, do you want children, mothers, brothers, sisters, lands? Renounce the primacy of your natural relationships, and follow Jesus into the fellowship of the people of God.

EUNUCHS FOR THE KINGDOM?

What shall we say then in view of this great biblical vision of the secondary and temporary nature of marriage and procreation? We will say what Jesus and Paul said. Jesus said in Matthew 19:12, "There are eunuchs who have been so from birth, and there are eunuchs who have been made eunuchs by men, and *there are eunuchs who have made themselves eunuchs for the sake of the kingdom of heaven*. Let the one who is able to receive this receive it." We need not take this ("made themselves eunuchs") to mean any kind of physical sterilization any more than we take Jesus' words "tear out your right eye" to mean physically blinding ourselves. But it does mean that Jesus approves some of his followers' renouncing marriage and sexual activity for the sake of serving Christ's kingdom. "Let the one who is able to receive this receive it."

That is what Paul chose for himself and what he encouraged others to consider in 1 Corinthians 7.

> To the unmarried and the widows I say that it is good for them to remain single as I am. . . . I want you to be free from anxieties. The unmarried man is anxious about the things of the Lord, how to please the Lord. But the married man is anxious about worldly things, how to please his wife. . . . I say this . . . to secure your undivided devotion to the Lord. (1 Cor. 7:8, 32–33, 35)

In other words, some are called to be "eunuchs" for the kingdom of God. Paul speaks about each having his own gift: "one of one kind, one of another" (1 Cor. 7:7). In other words, "Let the one who is able to receive this receive it" (Matt. 19:12).

BETTER BLESSINGS

So now we end where we began with all this Scripture in our mind. God promises those of you who remain single in Christ blessings that are better than the blessings of marriage and children.

Someone might ask, wouldn't it be better to have both—the blessings of marriage and the blessings of heaven? There are two answers to that question. One is that you will find out someday, and better to learn it now, that the blessings of being with Christ in heaven are so far superior to the blessings of being married and raising children that asking this question will be like asking, wouldn't it be better to have the ocean and also the thimbleful? But that's not the answer you wanted. So here is another one: Marriage and singleness both present us with unique trials and unique opportunities for our sanctification—our preparation for heaven. There will be unique rewards for each. Which is greater will not depend on whether you were married or single, but on how you responded to each.

So I say again to all singles in Christ, God promises you blessings in the age to come that are better than the blessings of marriage and children.

WHAT SINGLENESS SHOWS BEST

And with this promise, there comes a unique calling and a unique responsibility. It is not a calling to extend irresponsible adolescence into your thirties. It is a calling to do what only single men and women in Christ can do in this world, namely, to display by the Christ-exalting devotion of your singleness the truths about Christ and his kingdom that shine more clearly through singleness than through marriage. As long as you are single, this is your calling: to so live for Christ as to make it clearer to the world and to the church

1) that the family of God grows not by propagation through sexual intercourse, but by regeneration through faith in Christ;

2) that relationships in Christ are more permanent, and more precious, than relationships in families;

3) that marriage is temporary and finally gives way to the relationship to which it was pointing all along: Christ and the church—the way a picture is no longer needed when you see face-to-face; 4) and that faithfulness to Christ defines the value of life; all other relationships get their final significance from this. No family relationship is ultimate; relationship to Christ is.

Marriage has its unique potential for magnifying Christ that singleness does not have. Singleness has its unique potential for magnifying Christ that marriage does not have. To God be glory in the Christ-exalting drama of marriage and in the Christ-exalting drama of the single life.

The physical presence of other Christians is a source of incomparable joy and strength to the believer. . . . The prisoner, the sick person, the Christian in exile sees in the companionship of a fellow Christian a physical sign of the gracious presence of the triune God. Visitor and visited in loneliness recognize in each other the Christ who is present in the body; they receive and meet each other as one meets the Lord, in reverence, humility, and joy. . . . It is true, of course that what is an unspeakable gift of God for the lonely individual is easily disregarded and trodden under foot by those who have the gift every day.

DIETRICH BONHOEFFER,
Life Together, 8–9

CHAPTER TEN

SINGLENESS, MARRIAGE, AND THE CHRISTIAN VIRTUE OF HOSPITALITY

The end of all things is at hand; therefore be self-controlled and sober-minded for the sake of your prayers. Above all, keep loving one another earnestly, since love covers a multitude of sins. Show hospitality to one another without grumbling. As each has received a gift, use it to serve one another, as good stewards of God's varied grace: whoever speaks, as one who speaks oracles of God; whoever serves, as one who serves by the strength that God supplies—in order that in everything God may be glorified through Jesus Christ. To him belong glory and dominion forever and ever. Amen.

1 PETER 4:7–11

What's driving this chapter is a desire for Christ to be magnified in the way married people and single people show hospitality to each other. Or, to put it another way, if it's true, as I tried to show in the previous chapter, that God's family, which comes into being by regeneration, is more central and more lasting than the human family that comes into being by procreation, the implications for relationships are very important. How members of that family, the church, relate to each other as married and single will witness to the world that our lives are oriented on the supremacy of Christ and that our relationships are defined not just by nature, but by Christ. I long to see Christ magnified through married people folding single people into their lives and single people folding married people into their lives for the sake of Christ and the gospel.

"BECAUSE HE IS A DISCIPLE"

Jesus said, "Whoever gives one of these little ones even a cup of cold water *because he is a disciple*, truly, I say to you, he will by no means lose his reward" (Matt. 10:42). Of course, Jesus also said that we should love our *enemy* (Matt. 5:44), and Paul said to give a cup of water to our *enemy* (Rom. 12:20). That kind of love will receive its reward. But *here* Jesus says to show simple kindness to people precisely *because they are followers of Jesus*. And that too will receive its reward.

In other words, when you look into the eyes of a single person or a married person and you see the face of a follower of Jesus—a brother or a sister of your own eternal family—that relationship with Jesus that you see should draw out your heart in practical kindness—like hospitality—for Jesus' sake. Jesus is the focus here. He says to do this "*because he is my disciple.*" "I will be honored," he says, "in a special way if you give my disciple a drink for that reason. If you welcome him into your home, do this for my sake." That is what I mean when I say, I long to see *Christ* magnified through married people folding single people into their lives and single people folding married people into their lives.

WHY ARE THERE BODIES AND BIRDS AND BREAD AND WINE?

Just a few more words of introduction before we look at the text in 1 Peter. Thinking about the resurrection of the dead and the new heavens and the new earth has raised for me many questions about the material world. For example: Why did God give us bodies in the first place? Why did he make a material universe? Why does he raise our bodies from the dead and make them new and then liberate this earth so that it is a new earth where we can live forever in our new bodies? If God meant to have great praise ("Great is the LORD, and greatly to be praised," Ps. 96:4), why not just create angels with no bodies but great hearts who can only speak to God and not to each other? Why all these bodies, and why should persons be able to communicate with each other? And why trees and earth and water and fire and wind and lions and lambs and lilies and birds and bread and wine?

There are several deep and wonderful answers to these questions.

But the one I want to mention is this: God made bodies and material things because when they are rightly seen and rightly used, God's glory is more fully known and displayed. The heavens are telling the glory of God (Ps. 19:1). That's why the physical universe exists. Consider the birds of the air and the lilies of the field, and you will know more of God's goodness and care (Matt. 6:26–28). See in the things he has made his invisible attributes—his eternal power and divine nature (Rom. 1:20). Look at marriage and see Christ and the church (Eph. 5:23–25). As often as you eat this bread and drink this cup, you declare the Lord's death until he comes (1 Cor. 11:26). Whether you eat or drink or whatever you do, do all to the glory of God (1 Cor. 10:31). The material world is not an end in itself; it is designed to display God's glory and to awaken our hearts to know him and value him more.

MAKING FOOD AND SEX HOLY

Physical reality is good. God made it as a revelation of his glory. And he intends for us to sanctify it and worship him with it—that is, to see it in relation to him and to use it in a way that makes much of him and, in doing so, gives us joy. Knowing this protects us from idolizing sex and food as *gods*. They are not gods; they are made by God to honor him. And it protects us from fearing sex and food as *evil*. They are not evil; they are instruments of worship—they are ways to make much of Christ.

Here's the key text: 1 Timothy 4:1–5. It is one of the most important texts in the Bible on the meaning of physical appetites and sex.

> Now the Spirit expressly says that in later times some will depart from the faith by devoting themselves to deceitful spirits and teachings of demons, through the insincerity of liars whose consciences are seared, who forbid marriage and require abstinence from foods that God created to be received with thanksgiving by those who believe and know the truth. For everything created by God is good, and nothing is to be rejected if it is received with thanksgiving, for it is made holy by the word of God and prayer.

Sex and food—two great idols in first-century Asia Minor and twenty-first-century America. And God's response to those who solve the problem of the idolatry of sex and food by merely renouncing or avoiding them is to say these false teachers are demonic—devoting themselves to the "teachings of demons" (v. 1).

What is God's solution? Everything created by God is good; nothing is to be rejected if it is received with thanksgiving and made holy by the word of God and prayer. We make food holy by using it according to the word of God in Christ-dependent prayer. We make sex holy by using it according to the word of God in Christ-dependent prayer.

MAKING MUCH OF CHRIST—SINGLE OR MARRIED

All of that is simply introduction to make clear that neither marriage as a physical parable nor singleness as a physical parable is to be idolized or feared. Marriage is beautiful and physical. Singleness is beautiful and physical. God made them both. Both are designed, like all of nature, to display the glory of Christ.

Marriage *and* celibacy can be idolatrous. Spouses can worship each other or worship sex or worship their children or worship double-income-no-kid buying power. Singles can worship autonomy and independence. Singles can look on marriage as a second-class Christian compromise with the sexual drive. Married people can look upon singleness as a mark of immaturity or irresponsibility or incompetence.

But what I am trying to clarify is that there are Christ-exalting ways to be married, and there are Christ-exalting ways to be single. There are ways to use our bodies and our appetites in marriage and in singleness that make much of Christ.

THAT INFAMOUS SENTENCE

And I think I should say just one brief word about that infamous sentence in 1 Corinthians 7:9: "If they cannot exercise self-control, they should marry. For it is better to marry than to burn with passion." Remember, this is addressed explicitly to men *and* women (v. 8). And here is the one thing I want to say about it: When a person seeks to be married, knowing that as a single he or she would "burn with passion," it doesn't have to mean that marriage becomes a mere channel for the sex drive. Paul would never mean that in view of all the magnificent things he said about marriage in Ephesians 5.

Instead when a person marries—let me simply use the man as an example—he takes his sexual desire, and he does the same thing with it that we must *all* do with all our physical desires if we would make them means of worship: 1) he brings it into conformity to God's word; 2) he subordinates it to a higher pattern of love and care; 3) he transposes the music of physical pleasure into the music of spiritual worship, 4) he listens for the echoes of God's goodness in every nerve; 5) he seeks to double his pleasure by making her joy his joy; and 6) he gives thanks to God from the bottom of his heart because he knows and he feels that he never deserved one minute of this pleasure.

FINALLY, THE ISSUE OF HOSPITALITY

Now to the text quoted at the beginning of this chapter, 1 Peter 4:7–11. What's driving this chapter, believe it or not, is a desire for Christ to be magnified in the way married people and single people show hospitality to each other. We will walk through the text quickly with brief comments and then draw out simple and obvious implications—and pray that God would use this word to change us for his glory and our joy.

Verse 7: "The end of all things is at hand." Peter knows that with the coming of the Messiah the end of the ages has arrived (1 Cor. 10:11; Heb. 1:1–2). We do not await the last days. We are in the last days, and have been since the Messiah came the first time. The kingdom of God has come (Luke 17:21). And therefore the consummation of all things could sweep the world in a very short time.

Therefore, in the same way that Jesus taught us to be vigilant over our lives and to be watchful, so also Peter says, "Be self-controlled and sober-minded for the sake of your prayers" (1 Pet. 4:7). That is, cultivate a very personal relationship with the one you hope to see face-to-face at his coming. Don't be unfamiliar with Christ. You don't want to meet him as a stranger. Seek in prayer all the help you will need in these last days so that you may stand firm in days of great stress (Luke 21:36). Don't depend on your spontaneity to bring you to prayer. "Be self-controlled and sober-minded for the sake of your prayers."

Then verse 8 says, "Above all, keep loving one another earnestly, since love covers a multitude of sins." Love is paramount, and it will be needed all the more as the end draws near. Why? Because the pressures and stresses and tribulations of the last days will put relationships under tremendous stress. In these days we will need each other, and the world will be watching to see if we are real: "By this all people will know that you are my disciples, if you have love for one another" (John 13:35). Will we cover and bear and endure each other's faults and foibles, or will anger rule our hearts?

Verse 9 gives one form of that love, and it is significant that Peter mentions doing it without grumbling. "Show hospitality to one another without grumbling." If we are loving earnestly and love is covering a multitude of sins, then we will not grumble so easily, will we? Love covers much of what makes us grumble. So hospitality without grumbling is the calling of Christians in the last days. In the very days when your stress is high, and there are sins that need covering, and reasons to grumble abound—in those very days, Peter says, what we need to do is practice hospitality.

Our homes need to be open. Because our hearts are open. And our hearts are open because God's heart is open to us. Do you recall how the apostle John connected the love of God with our love for each other in relation to hospitality? He wrote in 1 John 3:16–17, "By this we know love, that [Jesus] laid down his life for us, and we ought to lay down our lives for the brothers. But if anyone has the world's goods and sees his brother in need [single or married!], yet closes his heart against him, how does God's love abide in him?"

WHAT HAPPENS IN OUR HOMES?

That's as far as we will go in 1 Peter 4:7–11, except simply to point to what happens when we get together in our homes. Verse 10: "As each has received a gift, use it to serve one another, as good stewards of God's varied grace." I love the phrase "stewards of God's varied grace"! Every

Christian is a steward—a custodian, a manager, a warden, a distributor, a servant—of God's varied grace. What a great reason to be alive! Every Christian lives on grace. "God is able to make all *grace* abound to you, so that having all sufficiency in all things at all times, you may abound in every good work" (2 Cor. 9:8). If you are afraid of hospitality—that you don't have much personal strength or personal wealth—good. Then you won't intimidate anybody. You will depend all the more on God's grace. You will look all the more to the work of Christ and not your own work. And what a blessing people will get in your simple home or your little apartment.

AS CHRIST HAS WELCOMED YOU

So there it is: the Christian virtue of hospitality—a Christ-exalting strategy of love in the last days. Now some closing applications. First, to everyone: If you belong to Christ, if you have by faith received his saving hospitality, which he paid for with his own blood, then extend this hospitality to others. Romans 15:7: "Welcome one another as Christ has welcomed you, for the glory of God." You live on free grace every day. Be a good steward of it in hospitality.

Second, to married couples. Plan that your hospitality will include single people—small groups, Sunday dinners, picnics, holiday celebrations. You would be surprised how many younger and older singles spend Christmas, Easter, and Thanksgiving alone. Everybody assumed someone else invited them. You don't need to make a big deal out of it. Just be natural. And don't forget that there are eighteen-year-old singles and eighty-year-old singles—and seventy- and sixty- and fifty- and forty- and thirty- and twenty-year-old singles, male and female, formerly married and never married, divorced and widowed. Think like a Christian. This is your family—more deeply and more eternally than your kinfolk.

Third, to single people. Show hospitality to other single people *and* to married couples and families. That may feel odd. But the oddness of it in this world may make it a greater witness to a truth that goes beyond this world. Would it not be a mark of unusual maturity and stability? Would it not be a mark of God's grace in your life? Would it not witness to the truth about what the ultimate family really is? Team up with some friends and invite married people into your lives.

I pray that the Lord would do this beautiful work among us—all of us. The end of all things is at hand. Let us be sober for our prayers. Let us love each other. Let us be good stewards of the varied grace of God, and let us show hospitality without grumbling. "Welcome one another as Christ has welcomed you."

Jesus does not enjoin his disciples to marry, but he does sanctify marriage according to the law by affirming its indissolubility and by prohibiting the innocent party from remarrying when the guilty partner has broken the marriage by adultery. This prohibition liberates marriage from selfish, evil desire, and consecrates it to the service of love, which is possible only in a life of discipleship. Jesus does not depreciate the body and its natural instincts, but he does condemn the unbelief which is so often latent in its desires. . . . Even our bodies belong to Christ and have their part in the life of discipleship, for they are members of his Body.

DIETRICH BONHOEFFER,
The Cost of Discipleship, 149–150

CHAPTER ELEVEN

Faith and Sex in Marriage

*Let marriage be held in honor among all, and let the marriage bed be
undefiled, for God will judge the sexually immoral and adulterous. Keep
your life free from love of money, and be content with what you have, for
he has said, "I will never leave you nor forsake you."*

HEBREWS 13:4–5

Before we turn to the place of childbearing and child-rearing, we
should consider the enormous importance of sexual relations in
marriage. We will see in the coming chapters that the duty to be fruitful
and multiply is not absolute. Nor are sexual relations bound exclusively
to the act of procreation. God did not make this massive capacity for
pleasure merely to make sure there would be a new generation. It works
that way. But God could have arranged it so that we get no pleasure in
it, but get nauseated if we don't have sex twice a week. That would have
worked too. There is more to this pleasure than procreation.

INCONCEIVABLE ECSTASIES

It is no accident that centuries of Bible scholars construed the Song of
Solomon as a story about Christ and the church. They may have been
too squeamish about letting it have its natural meaning for Solomon
and his bride, but they were not wrong in seeing that the ultimate
meaning of marital sex is about the final delights between Christ and
his church.

You don't have to be an ascetic, and you don't have to be afraid of
the goodness of physical pleasure, to say that sexual intimacy and sexual

climax get their final meaning from what they point to. They point to ecstasies that are unattainable and inconceivable in this life. Just as the heavens are telling the glory of God's power and beauty, so sexual climax is telling the glory of immeasurable delights that we will have with Christ in the age to come. There will be no marriage there (Matt. 22:30). But what marriage meant will be there. And the pleasures of marriage, ten-to-the-millionth power, will be there.

The pleasures we will experience there are of such a kind that if God tried to explain them to us now, it would be like trying to explain sexual pleasure to a five-year-old. The child might nod his head. But then he would say, "Pass the peanut butter." Sexual pleasures in marriage are good. If I were to tell you otherwise, the Bible would accuse me of spreading "teachings of demons." "In later times some will depart from the faith by devoting themselves to . . . *teachings of demons*, through the insincerity of liars . . . who forbid marriage and require abstinence from foods that God created to be received with thanksgiving by those who believe and know the truth" (1 Tim. 4:1–3). Woe to me if I do not celebrate the gift of sex in marriage.

THE PRIVATE SCENES IN THE DRAMA OF MARRIAGE

That celebration is not optional for the married. We are *commanded* to enjoy each other's bodies. "Let your fountain be blessed, and rejoice in the wife of your youth, a lovely deer, a graceful doe. Let her breasts fill you at all times with delight; be intoxicated always in her love" (Prov. 5:18–19). "Let him kiss me with the kisses of his mouth! For your love is better than wine" (Song 1:2). Husband and wife are meant to pursue the pleasures God has created for this relationship.

The world should not have its nose or its cameras in our bedroom. Sex is not a spectator sport—in spite of the billion-dollar industry designed to make it one. Which means that the drama of Christ and the church in the life of husband and wife has its private scenes. This part of the drama has an audience of three: husband, wife, and God, who sees all. Here the players of the drama watch as they are carried along on currents of pleasure. And if they would honor the meaning of this gift, they will marvel that this—even this, as intense as it may be—is but an emblem of something infinitely greater to come. The private scenes of the drama of Christ and his church are known in all the world. We would do well to tell the world what it is that they love so much. The love of Christ for his bride is not left without a witness anywhere.

WHEN SEX PROCEEDS FROM FAITH, IT IS NOT SIN

Turn with me now to reflect on the implications of Hebrews 13:4–5. "Let marriage be held in honor among all, and let the marriage bed be undefiled, for God will judge the sexually immoral and adulterous. Keep your life free from love of money." It is remarkable that the writer puts money and the marriage bed side by side. It is not a coincidence that most counselors today would put money and sexual relations near the top of their lists of trouble spots in marriage. Agreement in money matters and harmony in the marriage bed don't come easily. Our focus is on the marriage bed. But don't lose sight of how closely connected the two are. The pursuit of power and pleasure mingle in these two areas as in no others.

The writer is jealous to protect the marriage bed. He wants it to be good. He does not want it to be ruined. He exhorts, "Let the marriage bed be undefiled." He is not thinking about ceremonial defilements. We know that because he says, "God will judge the sexually immoral and adulterous." He is thinking about all sinful defilements. Ultimately, sin is anything that does not come from faith. That is what Paul says in Romans 14:23: "Whatever does not proceed from faith is sin." So the writer is saying: Guard sexual relations in marriage by not doing anything that does not come from faith.

Faith, he says in Hebrews 11:1, is "the assurance of things hoped for, the conviction of things not seen." In other words, faith is the confidence we feel in all that God promises to be and do for us in all the tomorrows of our lives. Now, how does such faith produce sexual attitudes and acts that are not sin? In the context, the writer shows us how this works in relation to money. We can then make the application to sex.

In Hebrews 13:5 he says, "Keep your life free from the love of money, and be content with what you have." The love of money is a desire that displeases God; it is sin. Now the antidote to this sinful love and all the evils that flow from it is contentment: "Be content with what you have." But the writer doesn't leave us there by ourselves to somehow crank up contentment. He goes on to give a basis for contentment: "For he [God] has said, 'I will never leave you nor forsake you.'" The basis for contentment is the promise of God's unfailing help and fellowship.

So the writer to the Hebrews is saying this: God has made such comforting, reassuring, hope-inspiring promises in his Word (like the one quoted here from Deuteronomy 31:6) that if we have faith in these promises, we will be content. And contentment is the antidote to the love of money and the antidote for all sexual sin.

Sin is what you feel and think and do when you are not taking God at his word and resting in his promises. So the command of Hebrews 13:4 can be stated like this: Let your sexual relations be free from any act or attitude that does not come from faith in God's word. Or to put it positively: Have those attitudes and do those acts in your marital sexual relations that grow out of the contentment that comes from confidence in God's promises.

IF I AM CONTENT IN CHRIST, WHY HAVE SEX?

But now immediately a problem emerges. Someone may ask, "If I am content through faith in God's promises, why should I even seek sexual gratification at all?" That is a very good question. And the first answer to it is: "Maybe you shouldn't seek any sexual gratification. Maybe you should stay single." We talked about that in Chapter 9.

But there is a second answer to this question, namely, the contentment that God's promises give does not mean the end of all desires, especially bodily desires. Even Jesus, whose faith was perfect, got hungry and desired food and got tired and desired rest. Sexual appetite is in this same category. The contentment of faith does not take it away any more than it takes away hunger and weariness. What, then, does contentment mean in relation to ongoing sexual desire?

I think it means two things. First, if gratification of that desire is

denied through singleness, then that denial will be compensated for
by an abundant portion of God's help and fellowship through faith.
In Philippians 4:11–13 Paul said, "Not that I am speaking of being in
need, for I have learned in whatever situation I am to be content. . . .
I have learned the secret of facing plenty and hunger, abundance and
need. I can do all things through him who strengthens me." If Paul
could learn to be content in hunger, then we can learn to be content if
God chooses not to give us sexual gratification.

Second, the other thing contentment means in relation to ongoing
sexual desire is this: If gratification is not denied us but is offered to us in
marriage, we will seek it and enjoy it only in ways that reflect our faith.
To put it another way, while the contentment of faith does not put an
end to our hunger, weariness, or sexual appetite, it does transform the
way we go about satisfying those desires.

Faith doesn't stop us from eating, but it stops gluttony; it doesn't
stop sleep, but it keeps us from being a sluggard. It doesn't stop sexual
appetite but . . . But what? That's what I want to deal with in the space
that's left.

WHAT WE ARE DOING IS NOT DIRTY

First, when the ear of faith hears the word from 1 Timothy 4:4–5—
"Everything created by God is good, and nothing is to be rejected if it
is received with thanksgiving, for it is made holy by the word of God
and prayer"—when the ear of faith hears that, it believes. And so faith
honors the body and its appetites as God's good gifts. Faith will not
allow a married couple to lie in bed and say to themselves, "What we
are doing is dirty; it's what they do in the pornographic movies." Instead
faith says, "God created this act, and it is good, and it is for 'those who
believe and know the truth'" (1 Tim. 4:3).

THE SCAR OF FORGIVEN SIN WILL NOT DESTROY

Second, faith increases the joy of sexual relations in marriage because
it frees us from the guilt of the past. I have in mind here those who are
married but have to look back on an act of fornication, or adultery,
or incest, or a homosexual fling, or years of habitual masturbation, or

preoccupation with pornography, or promiscuous petting, or divorce. And what God says is this: If it genuinely lies within you, by the grace of God, to throw yourself on the mercy of God for forgiveness, then he will free you from the guilt of the past. He will make a new, clean sexual life possible in marriage.

We are not naive. Even though the guilt of our sin can be washed away, some of the scars remain. I can imagine a couple, for example, just before their engagement sitting together in a park. He turns to her and says, "There is something that I have to say. Two years ago I had sex with another girl. I was away from the Lord; she was the only one. I've wept over it many times. I believe God has forgiven me, and I hope you can."

In the weeks that follow, not without tears, she forgives him, and they marry. And on their first honeymoon night, they lie together, and as he looks at her, the tears well up in her eyes, and he says, "What's the matter?" And she says, "I just can't help but think of that other girl, that she lay right here where I am." And years later, when the novelty of his wife's body has worn off, he finds himself inadvertently drifting back in his imagination to the illicit thrill of that first relationship. That's what I mean by scars. And all of us have similar scars of one kind or another. All of us have committed sins that, though forgiven, make our present life more problematic than if we hadn't committed them.

But I don't want to give the impression that Christ is powerless against such scars. He may not remove all the problems that these scars cause us, but he has promised to work even in all these problems for our good if we love him and are called according to his purpose (Rom. 8:28). Take our imaginary couple I just referred to. I prefer to think that there was a happy ending. They came eventually to a satisfying sexual relationship because they worked at it openly in constant prayer and reliance on the grace of God. They talked about all their feelings. They kept nothing bottled up. They trusted each other and helped each other, and they found their way to peace and sexual harmony and, above all, new dimensions of God's grace. Christ died not only that in him we might have guilt-free sexual relations in marriage, but also that he might then, even through our scars, convey to us some spiritual good.

DEFEATING SATAN WITH FREQUENT SEX

The third thing that we can say about faith and sexual relations in marriage is that faith uses sex against Satan. Consider 1 Corinthians 7:3–5:

> The husband should give to his wife her conjugal rights, and likewise the wife to her husband. For the wife does not have authority over her own body, but the husband does. Likewise the husband does not have authority over his own body, but the wife does. Do not deprive one another, except perhaps by agreement for a limited time, that you may devote yourselves to prayer; but then come together again, so that Satan may not tempt you because of your lack of self-control.

In Ephesians 6:16 Paul says we should ward off Satan with the shield of faith. Here he says to married people, "Ward off Satan with sufficient sexual intercourse. Don't abstain too long, but come together soon, so that Satan will gain no foothold."

Well, which is it? Do we guard ourselves from Satan with the shield of faith or the shield of sex? The answer for married people is that faith makes use of sexual intercourse as a means of grace. For the people God leads into marriage, sexual relations are a God-ordained means of overcoming temptation to sin (the sin of adultery, the sin of sexual fantasizing, the sin of pornography). Faith humbly accepts such gifts and offers thanks.

BEST SEX: WHEN HER JOY IS HIS AND HIS IS HERS

Notice something else in 1 Corinthians 7:3–5. This is very important. In verse 4 Paul says that the man and the woman have rights over each other's bodies. When the two become one flesh, their bodies are at each other's disposal. Each has the right to lay claim to the other's body for sexual gratification.

But what we really need to see is what Paul commands in verses 3 and 5 in view of these mutual rights. He does *not* say, "Therefore stake your claim! Take your rights!" He says, "Husband, give her the rights that belong to her! Wife, give him the rights that belong to him!" (v. 3). And in verse 4: "Do not refuse one another." In other words, he does not encourage the husband or wife who wants sexual gratification to seize it without concern for the other's needs. Instead, he urges both husband and wife to always be ready to give his or her body when the other wants it.

I infer from this and from Jesus' teaching in general that happy and fulfilling sexual relations in marriage depend on each partner aiming to give satisfaction to the other. If it is the joy of each to make the other happy, a hundred problems will be solved before they happen.

Husbands, if it is your joy to bring her satisfaction, you will be sensitive to what she needs and wants. You will learn that the preparation for satisfactory sexual intercourse at 10 P.M. begins with tender words at 7 A.M. and continues through the day as kindness and respect. And when the time comes, you will not come on like a Sherman tank, but you will know her pace and bring her skillfully along. Unless she gives you the signal, you will say, "Her climax, not mine, is the goal." And you will find in the long run that it is more blessed to give than to receive.

Wives, it is not always the case, but usually it seems that your husband wants sexual relations more often than you do. Martin Luther said he found twice a week to be ample protection from the Tempter.[1] I don't know if his wife, Katie, was up for it every time or not. But if you're not, give it anyway, unless there are extraordinary circumstances. I do not say to you husbands, "Take it anyway." In fact, for her sake, you may go without. The goal is to outdo one another in giving what the other wants (Rom. 12:10). Both of you, make it your aim to satisfy each other as fully as possible.

HOLY SEX: SATAN'S DEFEAT, CHRIST'S DISPLAY, AND OUR DELIGHT

"Let marriage be held in honor among all, and let the marriage bed be undefiled." That is, do not sin in your sexual relations. And that means, have only those attitudes, and do only those acts, that come from faith in God's hope-giving promises. We should all regularly ask ourselves:

---

[1]William Lazareth writes: "As to the recommended frequency of marital coitus, the hale and hearty spirit (if not the actual words) of Luther's sexual counsel is reflected in the humorous couplet traditionally ascribed to him: 'Twice a week, hundred-four a year / should give neither cause to fear.'" *Luther on the Christian Home* (Philadelphia: Muhlenberg Press, 1960), 226.

"Does what I am feeling or doing have its roots in the contentment of faith or in the anxious insecurity of unbelief? Do my cravings conform to the contentment of faith or contradict it?" Those questions will give you help in hundreds of little and big ethical decisions.

In summary, my aim has been to show the impact of faith on three aspects of sexual relations in marriage. First, faith believes God when he says that sexual relations in marriage are good and clean and should be received with thanksgiving by those who believe and know the truth. Second, faith increases the joy of sexual relations in marriage because it frees us from the guilt of the past. Faith believes the promise that Christ died for all our sins, that in him we might have guilt-free, Christ-exalting sexual relations in marriage. And finally, faith wields the weapon of sexual intercourse against Satan. A married couple gives a severe blow to the head of that ancient serpent when they aim to give as much sexual satisfaction to each other as possible. Is it not a mark of amazing grace that on top of all the pleasure that the sexual side of marriage brings, it also proves to be a fearsome weapon against our ancient foe?

This should not surprise us. Marriage at its exquisite peak of pleasure speaks powerfully the truth of covenant-keeping love between Christ and his church. And that love is the most powerful force in the world. It is not surprising then that Satan's defeat, Christ's glory, and our pleasure should come together in this undefiled marriage bed.

Marriage is more than your love for each other.
It has a higher dignity and power, for it is God's holy
ordinance, through which he wills to perpetuate the
human race till the end of time. In your love you see only
your two selves in the world, but in marriage you are
a link in the chain of the generations,
which God causes to come and to pass away to his glory,
and calls into his kingdom.

DIETRICH BONHOEFFER,
Letters and Papers from Prison, 27

MARRIAGE IS MEANT FOR MAKING CHILDREN . . . DISCIPLES OF JESUS: HOW ABSOLUTE IS THE DUTY TO PROCREATE?

Children, obey your parents in the Lord, for this is right. "*Honor your father and mother*" *(this is the first commandment with a promise),* "*that it may go well with you and that you may live long in the land.*" *Fathers, do not provoke your children to anger, but bring them up in the discipline and instruction of the Lord.*

EPHESIANS 6:1–4

I have tried to show from Scripture that the main meaning of marriage is to display the covenant-keeping love between Christ and his church. In other words, marriage was designed by God, most deeply and most importantly, to be a parable or a drama of the way Christ loves his church and the way he calls the church to love him. This is the most important thing for all husbands and wives to know about the meaning of their marriage.

A MAGNIFICENT THING

The key passage has been Ephesians 5:23–25:

> The husband is the head of the wife *even as Christ is the head of the church*, his body, and is himself its Savior. Now *as the church submits to Christ*, so also wives should submit in everything to their husbands.

Husbands, love your wives, *as Christ loved the church* and gave himself up for her.

Beware of being so familiar with this that it doesn't strike you as amazing. Where in all the world would anyone talk about marriage this way? In three verses, he says it three times:

- Verse 23: marriage: *even as Christ is the head of the church.*
- Verse 24: marriage: *as the church submits to Christ.*
- Verse 25: marriage: *as Christ loved the church.*

What is the most important meaning of marriage? It is found in the words: "*as* Christ . . . *as* the church . . . *as* Christ." The ultimate meaning of marriage is not in marriage itself. It is not in the husband and not in the wife and not in the offspring. The ultimate meaning of marriage is in "as Christ," "as the church," "as Christ." Marriage is a magnificent thing because it is modeled on something magnificent and points to something magnificent. And the love that binds this man and woman in marriage is a magnificent love because it portrays something magnificent—"as Christ loved the church" and "as the church submits to Christ." The greatness of marriage is not in itself. The greatness of marriage is that it displays something unspeakably great, namely, Christ and the church.

MARRIAGE IS FOR MAKING BABIES . . . DISCIPLES

Now what I want to add in this chapter is that marriage is for making children . . . disciples of Jesus. There is a double meaning in that title that I hope will help you remember the point. Marriage is for making children—that is, procreation. Having babies. This is not the main meaning of marriage. But it is an important one and a biblical one. But then I add the words *disciples of Jesus*. Marriage is for making children into disciples of Jesus. Here the focus shifts. This purpose of marriage is not merely to add more bodies to the planet. The point is to increase the number of followers of Jesus on the planet.

The effect of saying it this way is that couples who cannot conceive because of infertility can still aim to make children followers of Jesus.

God's purpose in making marriage the place to have children was never merely to fill the earth with people, but to fill the earth with worshippers of the true God. One way for a marriage to fill the earth with worshippers of the true God is to procreate and bring the children up in the Lord. But that's not the only way. When the focus of marriage becomes "Make children disciples of Jesus," the meaning of marriage in relation to children is not mainly "Make them," but "Make them *disciples.*" And the latter can happen even where the former doesn't.

WHERE WE'RE HEADING

But we are getting ahead of ourselves. Here's where we are going. First, I want us to see that God's original plan in creation was for men and women to marry and have children. Second, I want us to see that in the fallen world we live in, not only is marrying not an absolute calling on all people (as we have seen), but neither is producing children in marriage an absolute calling on all couples. It is normal, good, painful, glorious—but not absolutely required of all. Thirdly, we will focus on what Ephesians 6:1–4 says about how marriage becomes the means for making children disciples of Jesus.

HAVING CHILDREN IS GOD'S WILL

First, the meaning of marriage normally includes, by God's design, giving birth to children and raising them in Christ.

> Then God said, "Let us make man in our image, after our likeness. And let them have dominion over the fish of the sea and over the birds of the heavens and over the livestock and over all the earth and over every creeping thing that creeps on the earth." So God created man in his own image, in the image of God he created him; male and female he created them. And God blessed them. And God said to them, "Be fruitful and multiply and fill the earth and subdue it and have dominion over the fish of the sea and over the birds of the heavens and over every living thing that moves on the earth." (Gen. 1:26–28)

After the Flood, we read in Genesis 9:1, "God blessed Noah and his sons and said to them, 'Be fruitful and multiply and fill the earth.'" This was God's original design. Marriage is the place for making children and filling the earth with the knowledge of the Lord the way the waters cover the sea (cf. Hab. 2:14). That has never ceased to be a good thing. "Like arrows in the hand of a warrior are the children of one's youth. Blessed is the man who fills his quiver with them! He shall not be put to shame when he speaks with his enemies in the gate" (Ps. 127:4–5).

And in the New Testament, no one is more positive about children than Jesus himself. Mark 10:13–14 says, "They were bringing children to him that he might touch them, and the disciples rebuked them. But when Jesus saw it, he was indignant and said to them, 'Let the children come to me; do not hinder them, for to such belongs the kingdom of God.'" So from beginning to end, the Bible puts a huge value on having and raising and blessing children. At our church there are many large families. We affirm them! It is a magnificent calling. We will come back to this in a moment. This is one of the great meanings of marriage—to bear and raise children for the glory of God.

HAVING CHILDREN IS NOT ULTIMATE

But the second main point I want to make is that, while the meaning of marriage normally includes giving birth to children, this is not absolute. In this fallen, sinful age, in desperate need of knowing the Redeemer, *nature* by itself does not dictate when or whether to beget children. The decision about whether to conceive children is not ultimately a decision about what is natural, but about what will magnify the Redeemer, Jesus Christ.

In other words, there's an analogy between the singleness question and the children question. God said in Genesis 2:18, "It is not good that the man should be alone; I will make him a helper fit for him." So it sounds, at first, like marriage is *always* the way to go. Then the unmarried Paul says in 1 Corinthians 7:7, 26, "I wish that all were [single] as I myself am. But each has his own gift from God, one of one kind and one of another. . . . I think that in view of the present distress it is good for a person to remain as he is." So there are different gifts and different callings. Marriage is not absolute.

Now consider the analogy between that and having children. In the beginning, God said to mankind, "Be fruitful and multiply and fill the earth" (Gen. 1:28). That's normal. That's good. But it's not absolute any more than marriage is absolute. What is absolute is to pursue *spiritual* children, not natural children. Marriage is not absolutely for making children. But it is absolutely for making children followers of Jesus. Consider a few passages.

HAVING HUNDREDS OF CHILDREN

In Mark 10:29–30, Jesus says,

> "Truly, I say to you, there is no one who has left house or brothers or sisters or mother or father or *children* or lands, for my sake and for the gospel, who will not receive a hundredfold now in this time, houses and brothers and sisters and mothers and *children* and lands, with persecutions, and in the age to come eternal life."

Here Jesus shifts the absolute from having children biologically to having hundreds of children through the family of Christ and through spiritual influence. It might include adoption. It might include foster care. It might include making your home a place for backyard Bible clubs. It might include hospitality in a neighborhood where your home is every kid's favorite place. It might include your nursery job or your care for your nieces and nephews or the Sunday School class you teach. The point is: Marriage is not absolutely for making children; but it is absolutely for making children followers of Jesus one way or the other, directly or indirectly.

In Romans 9:8 Paul writes, "It is not the children of the flesh who are the children of God, but the children of the promise are counted as offspring." In other words, in God's kingdom, the duty of bringing "children of the flesh" into being is not absolute, but seeking to bring into being "children of God" is absolute.

In 1 Corinthians 4:15 Paul says, "Though you have countless guides in Christ, you do not have many fathers. For I became your father in Christ Jesus through the gospel." This is the most important family in the Christian life, and this is the main way we have children—

not by natural birth, but by supernatural birth. For many marriages they go together. But not for all.

One more verse on this point. Romans 16:13: "Greet Rufus, chosen in the Lord; also his mother, who has been a mother to me as well." Here is motherhood extending out beyond the son of birth to the son of affection and care. So I conclude that among Christians, mothering and fathering by procreation is natural and good and even glorious when Christ is in it. But it is not absolute. Aiming to bring spiritual children into being is absolute. Marriage is for making children. Yes. But not absolutely. Absolutely marriage is for making children followers of Jesus.

MAKING MARRIAGE A PLACE FOR MAKING DISCIPLES

Finally, let's focus on God's calling on marriage to be a place for making children followers of Jesus. We will focus in the rest of this chapter on both mother and father—and in the next chapter on the father, because the father gets special focus in Scripture. Here's the text again:

> Children, obey your parents in the Lord, for this is right. "Honor your father and mother" (this is the first commandment with a promise), "that it may go well with you and that you may live long in the land." Fathers, do not provoke your children to anger, but bring them up in the discipline and instruction of the Lord. (Eph. 6:1–4)

FIVE OBSERVATIONS

First, the father has a leading responsibility in bringing the children up in the discipline and instruction of the Lord. Notice that verse 1 says, "Children, obey your *parents*." Both. Not only *father* or only *mother*, but *parents*. But when the focus shifts from the duty of children to the duty of parents, the father is mentioned, not the mother. "*Fathers*, do not provoke your children to anger, but bring them up in the discipline and instruction of the Lord." So my first observation that we will unpack in the next chapter is that in marriage, fathers have a leading responsibility to bring up the children in the discipline and the instruction of the Lord.

Second, nevertheless, both mother and father are called to this together. Both are mentioned as the special object of the child's obedience. Verse 1: "Children, obey your *parents* [mother and father] in the Lord." You can hear this truth in Proverbs 6:20–21: "My son, keep your *father's commandment*, and forsake not your *mother's teaching*. Bind them on your heart always; tie them around your neck." And Paul reminded Timothy to hold fast to what his mother and grandmother had taught him as a child (2 Tim. 3:14; 1:5). So both mother and father bear responsibility in this marriage to bring the children up in the Lord, with dad having the leading responsibility.

Third, it is important that mother and father be united in this effort. It is not always possible because sometimes one spouse is not a believer. In that case, you do the best you can in finding practical common ground, for example, in the way the children are disciplined. But God's design is a united front. Both have one goal: This child is to grow up in "the discipline and instruction of the Lord"—grounded and shaped and permeated by the Lord, aiming to honor the Lord. God does not design that we be divided on this. The children need one united front coming from mom and dad. Don't confuse the children. Work through your differences of what to teach and how and when to discipline, and then stand united before the children. Don't let the children manipulate you against each other. Make that a hopeless ploy. God is one. Let parents be one.

This leads to the fourth observation. The most fundamental task of a mother and father is to show God to the children. Children know their parents before they know God. This is a huge responsibility and should cause every parent to be desperate for God-like transformation. The children will have years of exposure to what the universe is like before they know there is a universe. They will experience the kind of authority there is in the universe and the kind of justice there is in the universe and the kind of love there is in the universe before they meet the God of authority and justice and love who created and rules the universe. Children are absorbing from dad his strength and leadership and protection and justice and love; and they are absorbing from mom her care and nurture and warmth and intimacy and justice and love— and, of course, all these overlap.

And all this is happening before the child knows anything about God, but it is profoundly all about God. Will the child be able to recognize God for who he really is in his authority and love and justice because mom and dad have together shown the child what God is like? The chief task of parenting is to know God for who he is in his many attributes—especially as he has revealed himself in the person of Jesus and his cross—and then to live in such a way with our children that we help them see and know this multi-faceted God. And, of course, that will involve directing them always to the infallible portrait of God in the Bible.

Finally, God has ordained that both mother and father be involved in raising the children because they are husband and wife before they are mother and father. And what they are as husband and wife is where God wants children to be: As husband and wife, they are a drama of the covenant-keeping love between Christ and the church. That is where God wants children to be. His design is that children grow up watching Christ love the church and watching the church delight in following Christ. His design is that the beauty and strength and wisdom of this covenant relationship be absorbed by the children from the time they are born.

THE MAIN MEANING SERVES THE SECONDARY MEANING

So what turns out is that the deepest meaning of marriage—displaying the covenant love between Christ and the church—is underneath this other meaning of marriage—making children disciples of Jesus. It is all woven together. Good marriages make good places for children to grow up and see the glory of Christ's covenant-keeping love.

May the Lord give us a united focus on what really matters in marriage: husbands and wives loving like Christ and the church, and the children seeing it, and by God's grace, loving what they see.

It is from God that parents receive their children,
and it is to God that they should lead them.

DIETRICH BONHOEFFER,
Letters and Papers from Prison, 31

MARRIAGE IS MEANT FOR MAKING CHILDREN . . . DISCIPLES OF JESUS: THE CONQUEST OF ANGER IN FATHER AND CHILD

Children, obey your parents in the Lord, for this is right. "Honor your father and mother" (this is the first commandment with a promise), "that it may go well with you and that you may live long in the land." Fathers, do not provoke your children to anger, but bring them up in the discipline and instruction of the Lord.

EPHESIANS 6:1–4

The ultimate meaning of marriage—the ultimate purpose of marriage—is to dramatize on the earth the covenant-keeping love between Christ and his church. What we saw in the previous chapter was that this flesh-and-blood drama of the love between Christ and the church is the God-designed setting for making children—and for making them disciples of Jesus. These are two purposes for marriage. And the ultimate one creates the God-ordained setting for the secondary one. Ultimately, marriage is a flesh-and-blood drama of how Christ (dramatized by the husband) loves his church, and how the church (dramatized by the wife) is devoted to Christ. And this flesh-and-blood drama creates the setting—the physical, emotional, moral, spiritual nest—for the other purpose of marriage, namely, bringing children into the world and bringing them to Jesus.

EMPTY-NESTERS

In a missionary prayer letter I read as I was preparing this chapter, one of our veteran missionary families explained that both their children are married now. So under the parents' picture were the words "empty-nesters." Everybody in our culture knows the meaning of the term *empty-nester*. Behind it is the assumption that one of the meanings of marriage is to be a nest for the younger birds until they can fly and find their own worms and build their own nests. And if we are Christians, we say that the very essence of that nest is the flesh-and-blood drama created by a husband and a wife living and showing and teaching the covenant-keeping love between Christ and his church. That activity is the essence of the nest.

A FOCUS ON FATHERS

So the question in this chapter is: What is supposed to happen with children in this drama? What is supposed to happen to the children that God puts in this flesh-and-blood parable of his Son's love? What happens in this nest for the sake of the younger birds? In answering this question, the reason I will focus on fathers is that in the text quoted above, Paul begins by referring to *parents* in verse 1 and then shifts to a focus on *fathers* in verse 4.

Notice verse 1: "Children, obey your *parents* in the Lord." So clearly both of the parents are giving guidance and instruction that can be obeyed, because the children are told to obey their parents, both mother and father. In this nest, both mother and father are teaching and modeling and guiding and disciplining.

We might expect Paul to continue this united focus on parents and say, "*Parents*, do not provoke your children to anger, but bring them up in the discipline and instruction of the Lord." But that is not what he says in verse 4. He says, "*Fathers*, do not provoke your children to anger, but bring them up in the discipline and instruction of the Lord." So I made the point in the previous chapter that in marriage, and in this nest created by marriage, fathers have a leading responsibility in raising children. Not a sole responsibility, but a leading one.

The way I like to say it, as I said at the end of Chapter 7, is that if there is a problem with the children at the Piper household, and if Jesus knocks on the door, and Noël comes to the door, he is going to say, "Hello, Noël, is the man of the house home? We need to talk." Not that Noël bears no responsibility. But I bear the leading responsibility in seeing that the children are brought up in the discipline and instruction of the Lord.

HEADSHIP EXTENDED TO RAISING CHILDREN

This leading responsibility in raising the children is simply the natural continuation of the leading responsibility in relation to the wife. Back in Ephesians 5:23–25, Paul said, "The husband is the head of the wife even as Christ is the head of the church. . . . Husbands, love your wives, as Christ loved the church and gave himself up for her." God doesn't make the husband the leader in relationship to his wife and then make the wife the leader in relation to the children. We husbands bear the responsibility in both directions. If it were otherwise, the children would be confused. In fact, millions of children today *are* confused, and a host of personal and social problems can probably be traced to this confusion.

So when Paul says in verse 4, "Fathers, do not provoke your children to anger, but bring them up in the discipline and instruction of the Lord," he is simply extending the implications of headship into the sphere of parenting. The husband bears the leading responsibility for the upbringing of the children. That is what it means to be a married man: sacrificial, loving headship in relationship to our wives, and firm, tender leadership in relationship to the united task of raising our children in the Lord. So that is what we want to think about in this chapter. What does Ephesians 6:4 call a father to do? That question is worthy of its own book. But this is not it. So I am going to focus only on one part of verse 4, namely, the charge not to provoke our children to anger. This charge must be central since it is the one thing Paul chooses to mention.

WHY ANGER?

In Ephesians 6:4, Paul begins by saying that fathers should *not* do something. "Fathers, do not provoke your children to anger." Of all the things Paul could have encouraged fathers not to do, he chooses this one. Amazing. Why this one? Why not, don't discourage them? Or pamper them? Or tempt them to covet or lie or steal? Why not, don't abuse them? Or neglect them? Or set a bad example for them? Or manipulate them? Of all the things he could have warned fathers against, why this: "Fathers, do not provoke your children to anger"?

There Will Be Plenty of Anger

He doesn't tell us why. So let me guess from what I know of Scripture and life. I'll suggest two reasons. First, he warns against provoking anger because anger is the most common emotion of the sinful heart when it confronts authority. Dad embodies authority. Apart from Christ, the child embodies self-will. And when the two meet, anger flares. A two-year-old throws a tantrum, and a teenager slams the door—or worse.

So I think Paul is saying that there is going to be plenty of anger with the best of parenting, so make every effort, without compromising your authority or truth or holiness, to avoid provoking anger. Consciously be there for the child with authority and truth and holiness in ways that try to minimize the response of anger. We'll come back to how.

Anger Devours Other Emotions

The second reason Paul may focus on not provoking anger in our children is because this emotion devours almost all other good emotions. It deadens the soul. It numbs the heart to joy and gratitude and hope and tenderness and compassion and kindness. So Paul knows that if a dad can help a child not be overcome by anger, he may unlock his heart to a dozen other precious emotions that make worship possible and make relationships sweet. Paul is trying to help fathers do what he had to do with his spiritual children. Listen to the heart-language of 2 Corinthians 6:11–13: "We have spoken freely to you, Corinthians; our heart is wide open. You are not restricted by us, but you are restricted by your own affections. In return (I speak *as to children*) widen your hearts also."

NO EMOTIONAL BLACKMAIL

So what shall we say to dads about this matter of anger in our children? First, we should say that this verse may not be used as emotional blackmail by the children. Blackmail would say, "I am angry, Dad, so you must be wrong because the Bible says you are not supposed to make me feel like this." Some people never grow out of this childish self-centeredness: "My emotions are the measure of your love; so if I am unhappy, you are not loving me." We have all experienced this kind of manipulation. We know Paul does not mean that because Jesus himself made many people angry, and Jesus never sinned or failed to love perfectly. Since all children are sinners, therefore, even the best and most loving and tender use of authority will provoke some children sometimes to anger.

So the point of verse 4 is not that anytime a child is angry a father has sinned. The point is to warn fathers that there is a huge temptation to say things and do things and neglect things that will cause *legitimately avoidable* anger in our children. Most of us are aware of the obvious things to avoid: yelling, unjust and excessive punishment, hypocrisy, verbal putdowns, etc. But even more important than avoiding the obvious aggravators, we fathers should think about what kinds of preemptive things we can do that don't just avoid anger but diminish or remove anger. That's the real challenge.

GOD'S INITIATIVES AND DAD'S

Think of this: God has never done anything that should legitimately cause anger in any of his children. We are never warranted in getting angry at God. Ever. It happens. And we should admit it, and tremble, and repent, and turn back to humble trust in his sovereign goodness. But even though God has never done anything that legitimately provokes our anger at him, what *has* he done about the breakdown in our relationship with him? He has taken initiatives to heal it—initiatives that were infinitely costly to him.

Look back at what Paul says about overcoming anger in relationship to God's Fatherhood. This text is a model for us fathers about one of the most crucial strategies for overcoming anger in our children. In Ephesians 4:31–5:2 God, you could say, is speaking to his children: "Let all bitterness and wrath and anger and clamor and slander be put away from you, along with all malice. Be kind to one another, tenderhearted, forgiving one another. . . ." Now, so far, it is just a command: Don't be angry; be forgiving. But commands are powerless in and of themselves. What comes next is powerful: ". . . as God in Christ forgave you." So here is our Father in heaven sending his own Son ("God *in Christ* forgave you") to pay the price for our sinful anger. Our Father is not just telling us not to be angry; rather, at great cost to himself, he is overcoming *his* anger and *our* anger in the death of Jesus.

Then in the next verse, Ephesians 5:1, he says explicitly that he is playing the role of a Father in this: "Therefore be imitators of God, as beloved *children*." We are children of God if we are united to Christ by faith. He is our Father. He has taken very painful initiatives to overcome his wrath and our sin—our anger. We are infinitely loved by God in Christ. So, fathers, imitate your heavenly Father. Take initiatives, no matter how painful to you or how out of character they may feel, to prevent or diminish the anger of your children.

THE BATTLE IS IN DAD'S HEART FIRST

The point I am stressing is this: When Paul says in Ephesians 6:4, "Fathers, do not provoke your children to anger," don't just *stop* doing things that provoke anger; *start* doing things that prevent and overcome anger. Start doing things that awaken in the heart of a child other wonderful emotions so that they are not devoured by anger—the great emotion eater.

The main task in all this is that you overcome your own anger and replace it with tenderhearted joy. Joy that spills over onto your children. "Out of the abundance of the heart the mouth speaks" (Matt. 12:34). If the heart feels angry, the mouth will sound angry. When the mouth of dad is mainly angry, the tender emotions of a child are consumed. In other words, being the kind of father God calls us to be means being the kind of Christian and the kind of husband God calls us to be.

CHRIST CRUCIFIED FOR YOU IS THE KEY

Being a Christian means receiving forgiveness freely from God for all our failures and all our anger. It means letting the smile of God in Christ melt the decades of hard, numbing, emotionless, low-grade anger. And then we let that healing flow to others. "Let all . . . anger . . . be put away from you. . . . Be kind to one another, tenderhearted, forgiving one another, as God in Christ forgave you" (Eph. 4:31–32). God forgave you. God has been kind to you. God is tenderhearted to you. It is all because of Christ. Therefore, in Christ, by the Spirit, fathers, we can do this. We can put away anger, and we can forgive, and we can experience and awaken in our children tenderheartedness with a whole array of precious emotions that may have been eaten up by anger. Those emotions can live again. In you. And in your children.

"Fathers, do not provoke your children to anger." Be like God to them. What he did for us was very costly. He did not spare his own divine Son in order to rescue other children from his own wrath and from their own rebellious rage. God does not call us to do this before he does it for us. That's the gospel. Before he commands us to love the way he does (5:1), he forgives all our failures to love. Get this, fathers! I am not calling you to love your children like this *so that* you will have a Father in heaven who is for you. It's the other way around. I am telling you that God, by the sacrifice and obedience of his Son, Jesus, through faith alone, has *already* become totally for you. "If God is for us, who can be against us?" (Rom. 8:31).

And now, after becoming that kind of forgiving, supporting, tender, sacrificial Father to us fathers, he calls us: "Be imitators of God, as beloved children" (Eph. 5:1). Experience the fullness of God's tender and tough emotions. He overcome his wrath. He has forgiven our sin. And in him—if you will have it—there is healing for decades of soul-destroying anger.

What our children need from us is that we experience the fullness of God's offer of healing. Here is the dynamic of fatherhood: As God has forgiven you, forgive your wife and forgive your children (Eph. 4:32). Sever the root of the whole cycle of anger by savoring to the depths of your soul the preciousness of God's forgiveness and God's promises. Don't provoke your children to anger. Show them in your own soul how it can be replaced with tenderhearted joy.

Perhaps it is clear now again that the primary meaning of marriage creates the atmosphere where this anger-defeating love can happen. There is no tension between marriage as a display of Christ's covenant-keeping love and marriage as an anger-defeating place for discipling children. That covenant-keeping love is the same love that triumphs over anger. It is humble, sacrificial, servant love. Husbands love their wives as Christ loved the church (Eph. 5:25). That very Christ-shaped love is the tender love that opens the heart of children and delivers them from anger. It is a beautiful unity: first, marriage as the display of covenant-keeping love between Christ and his church, and second, marriage as the place where children taste and see and flourish in that very Christ-sustained, covenant-keeping love. The two are one.

God makes your marriage indissoluble.
"What therefore God has joined together,
let no man put asunder" (Matt. 19:6).
God joins you together in marriage; it is his act,
not yours. Do not confound your love
for one another with God.

DIETRICH BONHOEFFER,
Letters and Papers from Prison, 28

CHAPTER FOURTEEN

WHAT GOD HAS JOINED TOGETHER, LET NOT MAN SEPARATE: THE GOSPEL AND THE RADICAL NEW OBEDIENCE

And he left there and went to the region of Judea and beyond the Jordan, and crowds gathered to him again. And again, as was his custom, he taught them. And Pharisees came up and in order to test him asked, "Is it lawful for a man to divorce his wife?" He answered them, "What did Moses command you?" They said, "Moses allowed a man to write a certificate of divorce and to send her away." And Jesus said to them, "Because of your hardness of heart he wrote you this commandment. But from the beginning of creation, 'God made them male and female.' Therefore a man shall leave his father and mother and hold fast to his wife, and the two shall become one flesh.' So they are no longer two but one flesh. What therefore God has joined together, let not man separate." And in the house the disciples asked him again about this matter. And he said to them, "Whoever divorces his wife and marries another commits adultery against her, and if she divorces her husband and marries another, she commits adultery."

MARK 10:1–13

As we near the end of this book on marriage, it is fitting that we think together about the implications of the meaning of marriage for divorce and remarriage. For many of you who have walked through a divorce and are now single or remarried, or whose parents were divorced, or some other loved one, the mere mention of the word carries a huge weight of sorrow and loss and tragedy and disappointment and anger and regret and guilt. Few things are more painful than divorce. It cuts to the depths of personhood unlike any other relational gash. It is emotionally more heart-wrenching than the death of a spouse. Death is usually clean pain. Divorce is usually unclean pain. In other words, the enormous loss of a spouse in death is compounded in divorce by the ugliness of sin and moral outrage at being so wronged.

THE DEVASTATION OF DIVORCE

It is often long years in coming, and long years in the settlement and in the adjustment. The upheaval of life is immeasurable. The sense of failure and guilt and fear can torture the soul. Like the psalmist, night after night a spouse falls asleep with tears (Ps. 6:6). Work performance is hindered. People don't know how to relate to you anymore, and friends start to withdraw. You can feel like you wear a big scarlet *D* on your chest. The loneliness is not like the loneliness of being a widow or a widower or a person who has never been married. It is in a class by itself. (Which is one reason why so many divorced people find each other.)

A sense that the future has been devastated can be all-consuming. Courtroom controversy compounds the personal misery. And then there is the agonizing place of children. Parents hope against hope that the scars will not cripple the children or ruin their marriages someday. Tensions over custody and financial support deepen the wounds. And the awkward and artificial visitation rights can lengthen the tragedy over decades. And add to all of this that it happens in America to over four out of every ten married couples.

LOVING THE DIVORCED

There are two ways to respond lovingly and caringly to this situation. One is to come alongside divorced persons and stand by them as they grieve and repent of any sinful part of their own. Then we can stay by them through the transitions and help them find a way to enjoy the forgiveness and the strength for new obedience that Christ obtained when he died and rose again.

The other way to respond lovingly and caringly is to articulate a hatred of divorce, and why it is against the will of God, and do all we can biblically to keep it from happening. Compromises on the sacredness and lifelong permanence of marriage—positions that weaken the solidity of the covenant-union—may feel loving in the short run but wreak havoc for thousands over the decades. Preserving the solid framework of the marriage covenant with high standards may feel tough now but produces ten thousand blessings for future generations. I hope that both of these ways of loving and caring will flourish in our churches. These two ways of loving are not *either-or*. Both are happening month after month.

WHEN CHRIST DIVORCES, WE MAY

One of the reasons that I have emphasized the ultimate meaning of marriage so much in these chapters is that the meaning of marriage is such that human beings cannot legitimately break it. *The ultimate meaning of marriage is the representation of the covenant-keeping love between Christ and his church.* To live this truth, and to show this truth, is what it means, most deeply, to be married. This is the ultimate reason why marriage exists. There are other reasons, but this is the main one.

Therefore, if Christ ever abandons and discards his church, then a man may divorce his wife. And if the blood-bought church, under the new covenant, ever ceases to be the bride of Christ, then a wife may legitimately divorce her husband. But as long as Christ keeps his covenant with the church, and as long as the church, by the omnipotent grace of God, remains the chosen people of Christ, then the very meaning of marriage will include: *What God has joined, only God can separate.*

GETTING SERIOUS ABOUT SACREDNESS

I pray that one of the effects of this book will be to make us as a people profoundly serious about the sacredness of marriage. The world treats this diamond like just another stone. But in fact, marriage is sacred beyond what most people imagine. It is a unique creation of God, a dramatic portrayal of God's relation to his people, and a display of the glory of God's covenant-keeping love. Against all the diminished attitudes about marriage in the world—Jesus' world and our world—the Lord's words about marriage are breathtaking. This is the work of God, not man, and it does not lie in man's prerogative to end it.

JESUS KNOWS HIS MOSES

In Mark 10:1–13, the Pharisees came to Jesus and asked him, "Is it lawful for a man to divorce his wife?" That's the question. Today people don't even ask the question. It is assumed. It's not only lawful, but easy and cheap. Just google the word *divorce* and see what you get ("Easy Online Divorce," "Simple Divorce Online," "No-Fault Divorce, $28.95," "Easy Online Divorce, $299"). Let me say cautiously and seriously: Those who scorn the design of God and the glory of Christ and build their lives and businesses and whole industries around making divorce cheap and easy are under the wrath of God and need to repent and seek his forgiveness through Christ before it is too late.

Jesus knew that the Pharisees in general were an "adulterous generation" (Matt. 12:39). He knew how they defended their divorces. So he leads them to that very place and asks them in Mark 10:3, "What did Moses command you?" He takes them to Moses. But they should be careful here. Moses didn't just write Deuteronomy, which they are about to quote. He also wrote Genesis. In Mark 10:4 they say, "Moses allowed a man to write a certificate of divorce and to send her away." That's true. It's a reference to Deuteronomy 24:1.

What will Jesus say in response to this defense of divorce? Verse 5: Jesus says to them, "Because of your hardness of heart he wrote you this commandment." This is amazing. It implies, in other words, that there are laws in the Old Testament that are not expressions of God's will for all time, but expressions of how best to manage sin in a particular people at a particular time. Divorce is never commanded and never instituted in the Old Testament. But it was permitted and regulated—like polygamy was permitted and regulated, and like certain kinds of slavery were permitted and regulated. And Jesus says here that this permission was not a reflection of God's ideal for his people; it was a reflection of the hardness of the human heart. "Because of your hardness of heart he wrote you this commandment."

BACK TO CREATION

Then Jesus takes the Pharisees (and us) back to God's will in creation and quotes Genesis 1:27 and 2:24 and shows us the way it is supposed to be. Verses 6–8: "But from the beginning of creation, 'God made them male and female.' 'Therefore a man shall leave his father and mother and hold fast to his wife, and the two shall become one flesh.'"

That's the end of his Scripture quoting. Now the question is: What will he do with it? Clearly Jesus sees a tension between Deuteronomy 24 and Genesis 1–2. The *but* at the beginning of verse 6 ("But from the beginning of creation . . .") means: God's will about divorce in Genesis 1–2 is not the same as his will expressed in Deuteronomy 24.

So the question is: Which way will Jesus go? Will he say, "Well, there is still hardness of heart today, even in my disciples, and so Deuteronomy expresses God's will for my followers today"? Or will he say, "I am the Messiah, the Christ. The Son of Man has come into the world to gather a people who by faith in him and union with him display the true meaning of marriage in the way they keep their marriage covenant"? Will the emphasis fall on the fact that in the church there is still hardness of heart, or will the emphasis fall on the fact that the old has passed away and the new has come (2 Cor. 5:17)?

JESUS' THREE CONCLUSIONS

Jesus draws three conclusions in Mark 10:8–9. He says (1) in verse 8, "*So* they are no longer two but one flesh." In other words, since God said in Genesis 2:24, "They shall become one flesh," therefore Jesus concludes for his day and ours: "So they *are* [now] no longer two but one flesh." Marriage is that kind of union—very profound, just as Christ and the church are one body (Rom. 12:5).

Then (2) the second conclusion Jesus draws is that this union of one flesh is the creation—the work—of God, not man. He says in verse 9, "What therefore God has joined together . . ." So even though two humans decide to get married, and a human pastor or priest or justice of the peace or some other person solemnizes and legalizes the union, all of that is secondary to the main actor, namely, God. "What *God* has joined together . . ." God is the main actor in the event of marriage.

Then (3) Jesus draws the conclusion at the end of verse 9: "Let not man separate." The word translated "man" here ("Let not *man* separate") is not the word for male over against female, but the word for human over against divine. The contrast is: "If *God* joined the man and woman in marriage, then mere *humans* have no right to separate what he joined." That's Jesus' third conclusion from Genesis 1–2. Since God created this sacred union with this sacred purpose to display the unbreakable firmness of his covenant love for his people, it simply does not lie within man's rights to destroy what God created.

NO, IT IS NOT LAWFUL

That's the end of Jesus' conversation with the Pharisees about divorce. He has more to say to his disciples, but he is done with the Pharisees. They ask no more. He tells no more. They came with their question. Jesus gave his answer. They asked, "Is it lawful for a man to divorce his wife?" And Jesus answers, "What therefore God has joined together, let not man separate." No, it is not lawful. It contradicts the ultimate meaning of marriage.

Of course, someone might say, it has *always* contradicted the meaning of marriage—even when the permission of Deuteronomy was written. Good observation. But Jesus is not thinking that way. He is calling his followers to a higher standard than the compromise with hardness of heart in Deuteronomy.

THE NEW RADICAL OBEDIENCE

Jesus did not come simply to affirm the Mosaic law. He came to fulfill it in his own consuming, forgiving, justifying obedience and death, and then to take his ransomed and forgiven and justified followers into the higher standards that were really intended when *all* of Moses is properly understood. Remember Matthew 5:17: "Do not think that I have come to abolish the Law or the Prophets; I have not come to abolish them but to *fulfill* them." Then he gives six examples of what this radical obedience will look like in his disciples.

Here are just two of those examples: 1) "You have heard that it was said to those of old, 'You shall not murder.' . . . But I say to you that everyone who is angry with his brother will be liable to judgment" (Matt. 5:21–22). 2) "You have heard that it was said, 'You shall not commit adultery.' But I say to you that everyone who looks at a woman with lustful intent has already committed adultery with her in his heart" (Matt. 5:27–28). And there are four more like this in Matthew 5.

In other words, Jesus came not only to fulfill the law in his own work, he came to take his people to a radical understanding of the law and a radical obedience to the law that is not based on law but on himself, and therefore reflects the fullness of what God wills for us—and especially reflects the gospel, the covenant-keeping work of Christ at Calvary for his church. Marriage among Christians is mainly meant to tell the truth about the gospel—that Christ died for his church who loves him and never breaks his covenant with his bride.

In essence, Jesus says, "You have heard that it was said, 'You are permitted to divorce.' But I say to you, 'I have come to conquer the hardness of your heart. I have come to die for your sins. I have come to count you as righteous. I have come to show you the drama that marriage was meant to represent in my sacrificial, covenant-keeping love for my sinful bride. I have come to give you the power to stay married, or to stay single, so that either way you keep your promises and show what my covenant is like and how sacred is the covenant bond of marriage.'"

So when the Pharisees are gone and Jesus is in the house with his disciples, he puts the matter even more bluntly and more radically. Mark 10:10–12: "And in the house the disciples asked him again about this matter. And he said to them, 'Whoever divorces his wife and marries another commits adultery against her, and if she divorces her husband and marries another, she commits adultery.'"

THE GOOD NEWS OF GRACE IN JESUS' RADICAL COMMAND

Mark does not report how stunned the disciples were at these words. Matthew does. I will try to show in the next chapter from two important passages in Matthew (5:32; 19:9) and three in 1 Corinthians (7:10–11, 12–16, 39) and one in Romans (7:1–3) why I think we should take Jesus at face value here and counsel against all remarriage after divorce while the spouse is living. That's what I think Jesus calls us to as his followers. Keep your marriage vows in such a way as to tell the truth about the unbreakable covenant love of Christ.

But to close this chapter, I want to emphasize that what Jesus says here in Mark 10:10–12 is incredibly good news—even to those who have been divorced and are remarried. Here's why: Jesus says, "Don't divorce your spouse and marry someone else. If you do, you've committed adultery." Why is it adultery? *Ultimately*, it is adultery because it betrays the truth about Christ that marriage is meant to display. Jesus never, never does that to his bride, the church. He never forsakes her. He never abandons her. He never abuses her. He always loves her. He always takes her back when she wanders. He always is patient with her. He always cares for her and provides for her and protects her and, wonder of wonders, delights in her. And you—you who are married once, married five times, married never—if you repent and trust Christ—receive him as the Treasure who bore your punishment and became your righteousness—you are in the bride. And that is how he relates to you. "Everyone who believes in him receives forgiveness of sins through his name" (Acts 10:43).

The radical call of Jesus never to divorce and remarry is a declaration of the gospel by which people who have failed may be saved. If Christ were not this way, we would all be undone. But this is how true, how faithful, how forgiving he is. Therefore, we are saved.

God makes your marriage indissoluble, and protects it
from every danger that may threaten it from within and
without; he will be the guarantor of its indissolubility.
It is a blessed thing to know that no power on earth,
no temptation, no human frailty can dissolve
what God holds together; indeed, anyone who knows
that may say confidently: What God has joined together,
can no man put asunder. Free from all the anxiety
that is always a characteristic of love, you can now say
to each other with complete and confident assurance:
We can never lose each other now;
by the will of God we belong to each other till death.

DIETRICH BONHOEFFER,
Letters and Papers from Prison, 28

CHAPTER FIFTEEN

WHAT GOD HAS JOINED TOGETHER, LET NOT MAN SEPARATE: THE GOSPEL AND THE DIVORCED

And Pharisees came up to him and tested him by asking, "Is it lawful to divorce one's wife for any cause?" He answered, "Have you not read that he who created them from the beginning made them male and female, and said, 'Therefore a man shall leave his father and his mother and hold fast to his wife, and the two shall become one flesh'? So they are no longer two but one flesh. What therefore God has joined together, let not man separate." They said to him, "Why then did Moses command one to give a certificate of divorce and to send her away?" He said to them, "Because of your hardness of heart Moses allowed you to divorce your wives, but from the beginning it was not so. And I say to you: whoever divorces his wife, except for sexual immorality, and marries another, commits adultery." The disciples said to him, "If such is the case of a man with his wife, it is better not to marry." But he said to them, "Not everyone can receive this saying, but only those to whom it is given. For there are eunuchs who have been so from birth, and there are eunuchs who have been made eunuchs by men, and there are eunuchs who have made themselves eunuchs for the sake of the kingdom of heaven. Let the one who is able to receive this receive it."

MATTHEW 19:3–12

I said in the previous chapter that there are two ways to be compassionate and caring in relation to divorce—not at all meaning that you choose between them, but that we must pursue both. One is to come alongside divorced persons while they grieve and (wherever necessary) repent, and to stay by them through the painful transitions, and to fold them into our lives, and to help them find a way to enjoy the forgiveness and the strength for new kinds of obedience that Christ has already obtained for them when he died and rose again. That's one way to love. And I pray we will all pursue it. The other way to respond with care and compassion is to articulate hatred for divorce, and why it is against the will of God, and to do all we can biblically to keep it from happening.

STAYING SINGLE TO SHOW THE TRUTH

One of the reasons I have included two chapters on the dignity and worth and Christ-exalting potential of singleness, even though this is a book on marriage, is that I know divorce throws thousands of people into that situation, many of them against their will. If we are going to stand for marriage as *the lifelong commitment to one living spouse*, then we must be prepared to love single, divorced people with all our hearts and homes and families.

We must keep a clear, biblical, eternal perspective and remind ourselves repeatedly that compared to eternal life with God, this earthly life—single or married, divorced or not—is very short. James says, "You are a mist that appears for a little time and then vanishes" (James 4:14). If a person is going to remain single to honor his or her marriage vows, that perspective will be crucial.

GOD MAKES AND GOD BREAKS

In Chapter 14 I took the stand that if the ultimate meaning of marriage is to represent the unbreakable covenant-love between Christ and his church (Eph. 5:22–33), then no human being has a right to break a marriage covenant. When the impossible day comes that Christ breaks his vow, "I am with you always, to the end of the age" (Matt. 28:20), then, on that day, a human being may break his marriage covenant.

This explains why Jesus does not settle for the divorce provision of Deuteronomy 24:1–4 (Mark 10:3–9) but says, "What therefore God has joined together, let not man separate" (Mark 10:9). In other words, since God is the one who decisively *makes* every marriage, only God has the right to *break* a marriage. And he does it by death. Which is why the traditional and biblical marriage vows have one and only one limitation: "Till death do us part," or "As long as we both shall live."

FOUR PRESSING QUESTIONS

As you know, when a person takes such a stand on the inviolability and sacredness of marriage, and the illegitimacy of divorce and remarriage while the spouses are alive, there are many questions, both biblical and practical, that have to be answered. So what I want to do in this chapter is to try to answer some of the more pressing ones.

1) Does death end a marriage in such a way that it is legitimate for a spouse to remarry? The answer is yes, and no one has seriously questioned this. One key text is Romans 7:1–3:

> Do you not know, brothers—for I am speaking to those who know the law—that the law is binding on a person only as long as he lives? For a married woman is bound by law to her husband while he lives, but if her husband dies she is released from the law of marriage. Accordingly, she will be called an adulteress if she lives with another man while her husband is alive. But if her husband dies, she is free from that law, and if she marries another man she is not an adulteress.

In other words, Paul says that to divorce and remarry while your spouse is living is adulterous, but to remarry after the death of a spouse is not. I think the reason for this is that Jesus made plain that in the resurrection there is no marriage (Matt. 22:30). So if a person said it was wrong to remarry after the death of a spouse, it would seem to imply that marriage is valid beyond death and in the resurrection. But it's not. Death is the decisive and eternal end of marriage. The spouse who has died has moved out of the earthly sphere where marriage happens and is no longer married. And therefore the spouse on earth is no longer married. Therefore, remarriage after the death of a spouse is not only legitimate, but it speaks a clear biblical truth—after death there is no marriage.

2) If a divorced person has already married again, should he or she leave the later marriage? The reason this question comes with such force is that Jesus speaks of the second marriage as committing adultery. Jesus says in Luke 16:18, "Everyone who divorces his wife and marries another commits adultery, and he who marries a woman divorced from her husband commits adultery."

My answer is that remarriage, while a divorced spouse is still living, is an act of unfaithfulness to the marriage covenant. In that sense, to remarry is adultery. We promised, "Till death do us part" because that is what God says marriage is, and even if our spouse breaks his or her covenant vows, we will not break ours.

But I do not think that a person who remarries against God's will, and thus commits adultery in this way, should later break the second marriage. The marriage should not have been done, but now that it is done, it should not be undone by man. It is a real marriage. Real covenant vows have been made. And that real covenant of marriage may be purified by the blood of Jesus and set apart for God. In other words, I don't think that a couple who repents and seeks God's forgiveness and receives his cleansing should think of their lives as ongoing adultery, even though, in the eyes of Jesus, that's how the relationship started. There are several reasons why I believe this.

First, in Deuteronomy 24:1–4, where the permission for divorce was given in the law of Moses, it speaks of the divorced woman being "defiled" in the second marriage so that it would be an abomination for her to return to her first husband, even if her second husband died. This language of defilement is similar to Jesus' language of adultery. And yet the second marriage stood. It was defiling in some sense, yet it was valid.

Another reason I think remarried couples should stay together is that when Jesus met the woman of Samaria, he said to her, "You have had five husbands, and the one you now have is not your husband" (John 4:18). When Jesus says, "The one you have now is not your husband," he seems to imply that the other five *were*. Not that it's right to divorce and marry five times. But the way Jesus speaks of it sounds as though he saw them as real marriages. Illicit. Adulterous to enter into, but real. Valid.

The third reason I think remarried couples should stay together is that even vows that should not be made, once they are made, should generally be kept. I don't want to make that absolute for every conceivable situation, but there are passages in the Bible that speak of vows being made that should *not* have been made, but they were right to keep (like Joshua's vow to the Gibeonites in Joshua 9). God puts a very high value on keeping our word, even when it gets us in trouble ("[The godly man] swears *to his own hurt* and does not change," Ps. 15:4). In other words, it would have been more in keeping with God's revealed will not to remarry, but adding the sin of another covenant-breaking does not please God more.[1]

There are marriages in the church I serve that are second marriages for one or both partners, which, in my view, should not have happened, but are today godly marriages—marriages that are clean and holy, and in which forgiven, justified husbands and wives please God by the way they relate to each other. As forgiven, cleansed, Spirit-led followers of Jesus, they are not committing adultery in their marriages. These marriages began as they should not have but have become holy.

3) If an unbelieving spouse insists on leaving a believing spouse, what should the believing spouse do? Paul's answer in 1 Corinthians 7:12–16 goes like this:

> To the rest I say (I, not the Lord [*which I think means, I don't have a specific command from the historical teachings of Jesus, but I am led by his Spirit, vv. 10, 12, 25, 40*]) that if any brother has a wife who is an unbeliever, and she consents to live with him, he should not divorce her. If any woman has a husband who is an unbeliever, and he consents to live with her, she should not divorce him. For the unbelieving husband is made holy because of his wife, and the unbelieving wife is made holy because of her husband. Otherwise your children would be unclean, but as it is, they are holy. [*Which I take to mean that marriage is such a holy union in God's eyes that a believer, a child of God, is not defiled by having sexual relations with an enemy of the cross; and the children are not born with any kind of special contamination because the father or mother is an enemy of Christ. They're not saved by*

---

[1] The imposed divorces of Ezra 10:6ff. are an exception to this rule that is probably owing to the unique situation of ethnic Israel under the old covenant living among idolatrous pagan peoples and breaking God's law not to intermarry with them. We know from 1 Corinthians 7:13 and 1 Peter 3:1–6 that the Christian answer to mixed marriages between a Christian and a non-Christian is not divorce.

being married to a believer or born to a believer, but they are set apart for proper and holy use in the marriage.]² But if the unbelieving partner separates, let it be so. In such cases the brother or sister is not enslaved. God has called you to peace. For how do you know, wife, whether you will save your husband? Or how do you know, husband, whether you will save your wife?

So the answer of this passage is that if divorce is forced on a believer by an unbeliever, the believer should not make war on the unbeliever to make the unbeliever stay. The reason Paul gives for this is in verse 15: "God has called you to peace." I do not believe this text teaches that we are free to remarry when this happens. Some take the words "In such cases the brother or sister is not enslaved" to mean "is free to remarry." There are several reasons why I don't think it means that.

First, when Paul says in verse 15, "In such cases the brother or sister is not enslaved [or bound]," I think he means "not enslaved to stay married when the unbeliever over time insists on leaving and sues for divorce." He's not saying, "The brother or sister is not enslaved to stay single—and is thus free to remarry," because Paul, the lover of singleness, would not have spoken of singleness as a state of slavery or bondage. It is very unlikely that Paul would talk like that.

The second reason I don't think he is saying the abandoned spouse is free to remarry is that he just pointed us in the opposite direction in verses 10–11: "To the married I give this charge (not I, but the Lord): the wife should not separate from her husband (but if she does, she should remain unmarried or else be reconciled to her husband), and the husband should not divorce his wife." With a statement like that in front of me ("if she does, she should remain unmarried or else be reconciled to her husband"), I am not inclined to think Paul is supporting remarriage four verses later.

The third reason I don't think he is supporting remarriage when he says "the brother or sister is not enslaved" is that Paul's argument in the next verse (v. 16) doesn't support that. It supports freedom to accept divorce peacefully, not freedom to remarry. Verse 16 says, "For how do

---

²I found Paul K. Jewett's *Infant Baptism and the Covenant of Grace* (Grand Rapids, MI: Eerdmans, 1978), 122–138 to be very helpful on this passage.

you know, wife, whether you will save your husband? Or how do you know, husband, whether you will save your wife?" In other words, you *don't* know, and therefore you can't use that as an argument to create a fight to stay married. So the words in verse 15, "In such cases the brother or sister is not enslaved," mean you are not enslaved to this marriage when your unbelieving spouse demands out, because you have no assurance that fighting to stay in will save him.

And a fourth reason for believing Paul upholds Jesus' ideal of no remarriage after divorce while the estranged spouse is alive is verse 39: "A wife is bound to her husband *as long as he lives*. But if her husband dies, she is free to be married to whom she wishes, only in the Lord." So it seems to me that Paul and Jesus are of one mind that followers of Jesus are radically devoted to one husband or one wife as long as they both shall live. This ideal tells the gospel truth most clearly: Christ died for his bride and never forsakes her.

4) Are there no exceptions to the prohibition of remarriage while the spouse is living?

My answer is no. But I am very much in the minority of biblical students, and even among Bible-believing scholars and pastors. I have tried to give extended biblical foundation for this view in two other places,[3] and so I won't go into a detailed defense here. We will simply turn briefly to Matthew 19 to address the main argument for lawful divorce and remarriage in cases of adultery.

"THE EXCEPTION CLAUSE"

Matthew 19:3–12 is very much like the words of Jesus we saw in Mark 10:1–12. There are two main differences. The first one is in verse 9 where there is an exception clause: "And I say to you: whoever divorces his wife, *except for sexual immorality*, and marries another, commits adultery." Most scholars say that the words "except for sexual immorality" mean that if there has been adultery, the aggrieved spouse is free to divorce and remarry.

---

[3]See Chapters 40–42 in John Piper, *What Jesus Demands from the World* (Wheaton, IL: Crossway Books, 2006), 301–322. See also "Divorce and Remarriage: A Position Paper" (July 21, 1986) at http://www.desiringgod.org/ResourceLibrary/Articles/ByDate/1986/1488_Divorce_and_Remarriage_A_Position_Paper/; accessed 04-25-08.

IS THAT WHAT JESUS MEANT?

I don't think that is what Jesus meant. Jesus does not use the word "adultery" (*moicheia*) here (when he says "except for sexual immorality"). He does not say "except for adultery," which is what we would expect him to say if he were referring to adultery. He does use the word for adultery elsewhere (Matt. 15:19), and he uses it specifically in distinction to the word he uses here, namely, the word that ordinarily means "fornication" (*porneia*, see especially John 8:41) when distinguished from adultery. Therefore, I think what Jesus is doing is warning his readers that this absolute prohibition against remarriage does not apply to the situation of betrothal, where fornication may have happened. In other words, he is saying, "When you hear me give an absolute prohibition of remarriage after divorce, don't include in that prohibition the divorce of a betrothed couple because of fornication."

Matthew is the one Gospel that tells about Joseph's intention to "divorce" his betrothed Mary because he thought she had committed fornication. "Her husband Joseph, being a just man and unwilling to put her to shame, resolved to *divorce* her quietly" (Matt. 1:19). The word for "divorce" here (*apolusai*) is the same as in Matthew 19:9. Moreover, Matthew says that Joseph was "just" or "righteous" (*dikaios*) in resolving to "divorce" Mary. There is no suggestion that Joseph would have been prohibited from marrying someone after "divorcing" Mary in this betrothed situation. My conclusion is that in Matthew 19:9, the inspired apostle is showing us that Jesus' prohibition of remarriage does not apply to Joseph's kind of situation.

This view is not widely held. I commend it for your serious consideration. It seems to me that the coming of Jesus into the world, and the beginning of the last days, and the outpouring of the Holy Spirit, and the inauguration of the kingdom of God, and the promised presence of the living Christ, and the radical nature of his commands point toward an elevation of expectation for his new-covenant people in this crooked and passing world. That is what I pray toward and preach toward.

CHRIST CRUCIFIED FORMS MARRIAGE AND SAVES SINNERS

Whether you agree with me concerning the grounds of divorce and remarriage or not, I pray that we will all recognize the deepest and highest meaning of marriage—not sexual intimacy, as good as that is, not friendship, or mutual helpfulness, or childbearing, or child-rearing, but the flesh-and-blood display in the world of the covenant-keeping love between Christ and his church. That is what I pray you will pursue, in your marriage or your singleness.

Through the gospel God gives us the power we need to love each other in this covenant-keeping way. We know this because in Matthew 19:11, after his radical call to faithfulness in marriage, Jesus said, "Not everyone can receive this saying, but only those to whom it is given." It *is* given to those who follow Christ. We are not left alone. He is with us to help us. If we have been sinned against, he will make it right sooner or later (Rom. 12:19). He will give us the grace to flourish while we wait. And if we have sinned, he will give the grace to repent and receive forgiveness and move forward in radical new obedience.

The gospel of Christ crucified for our sins is the foundation of our lives. Marriage exists to display it. And when marriage breaks down, the gospel is there to forgive and heal and sustain until he comes, or until he calls.

CONCLUSION:
THIS MOMENTARY MARRIAGE

I have said nothing about the effect of marriage on poverty, or health, or employment, or earnings, or the material success of children. The reason for this omission is not that marriage isn't significant for these things. It is enormously significant. "Marriage is an issue of paramount importance if we wish to help the most vulnerable members of our society: the poor, minorities, and children."[1]

The reason for the omission is different: Focusing on the pragmatic effects of marriage undermines the very power of marriage to achieve the effects we desire. In other words, for the sake of all these beneficial practical effects, we should not focus on them. This is the way life is designed by God to work. Make him and the glory of his Son central, and you get the practical effects thrown in. Make the practical effects central, and you lose both.

Of course, there are unbelievers whose marriages last and who prosper materially. But the personal dynamics that hold them together are rooted more deeply in God's design than they know. They do not look into each other's eyes and say, "Loving you was a shrewd financial transaction." Crass materialism sustains very few marriages. The vestiges of God's vision for marriage remain. They may be distorted and nameless, but they still remain. God's common grace grants many cut flowers to flourish for a lifetime.

So my concluding plea is not offered in ignorance of the importance of the material benefits of marriage. I want people to flourish in every way. I want the poor to rise into joyful, self-sustaining, productive work and stable households. Therefore, for the sake of these good effects of marriage, let it be heralded with joy that there are reasons for marriage that are vastly more important.

---

[1] Juan Williams, *Enough* (New York: Three Rivers Press, 2006), 216.

Marriage is not mainly about prospering economically; it is mainly about displaying the covenant-keeping love between Christ and his church. Knowing Christ is more important than making a living. Treasuring Christ is more important than bearing children. Being united to Christ by faith is a greater source of marital success than perfect sex and double-income prosperity.

If we make secondary things primary, they cease to be secondary and become idolatrous. They have their place. But they are not first, and they are not guaranteed. Life is precarious, and even if it is long by human standards, it is short. "What is your life? For you are a mist that appears for a little time and then vanishes" (James 4:14). "Do not boast about tomorrow, for you do not know what a day may bring" (Prov. 27:1).

So it is with marriage. It is a momentary gift. It may last a lifetime, or it may be snatched away on the honeymoon. Either way, it is short. It may have many bright days, or it may be covered with clouds. If we make secondary things primary, we will be embittered at the sorrows we must face. But if we set our face to make of marriage mainly what God designed it to be, no sorrows and no calamities can stand in our way. Every one of them will be, not an obstacle to success, but a way to succeed. The beauty of the covenant-keeping love between Christ and his church shines brightest when nothing but Christ can sustain it.

Very soon the shadow will give way to Reality. The partial will pass into the Perfect. The foretaste will lead to the Banquet. The troubled path will end in Paradise. A hundred candle-lit evenings will come to their consummation in the marriage supper of the Lamb. And this momentary marriage will be swallowed up by Life. Christ will be all and in all. And the purpose of marriage will be complete.

To that end may God give us eyes to see what matters most in this life. May the Holy Spirit, whom he sends, make his crucified and risen Son the supreme Treasure of our lives. And may that Treasure so satisfy our souls that the root of every marriage-destroying impulse is severed. And may the marriage-watching world be captivated by the covenant-keeping love of Christ.

A Few Words of Thanks

I waited forty years to write this book. There have been so many stresses in our marriage that I felt unfit to write about marriage at ten, twenty, or thirty years into it. Now at forty years, I realize we will never have it all together, so it seemed a good time to speak.

With the words of Paul ringing in my ears, "Let anyone who thinks that he stands take heed lest he fall" (1 Cor. 10:12), I say with some confidence now that I believe this marriage will last till one of us is dead. Judging by the paucity of widowers in our church, that will probably be me.

So let me say it while I still have breath: Thank you, Noël, for hanging in there for forty years. Thank you for making this book possible. I could not have written it without you. What I have seen in the Bible, we have forged in the furnace of life—forty years of marriage and thirty-six years of parenting. I love you.

Thank you, Karsten and Benjamin and Abraham and Barnabas and Talitha, for letting us experiment on you with our first marriage. We get no second chances. *You* are our second chances. We pray that you will do it better for being aware of our failings.

Thank you, Bethlehem Baptist Church, for loving us and praying for us for twenty-eight of these forty years, and for supporting our marriage and parenting during the hardest and best of times (which were sometimes the same). There is no place I would have rather spent our lives or raised our children.

Thank you to our parents, Ruth and Bill Piper and George and Pamela Henry, who gave us a rock-solid place to stand and a hundred good examples. They make the negative ones pale. Above all, thank you for telling us and showing us the gospel of Jesus Christ. There is no greater legacy than Christ.

Thank you to friends like David and Karin Livingston and Tom and Julie Steller who know our flaws perhaps as well as any and gave us their heart and their ears in the hardest seasons.

Thank you to my assistant David Mathis, whose proactive planning and burden-lifting set me free to think and pray and write when the time comes. Thank you, David, for working through the manuscript with me more than once and making so many good suggestions.

Thank you, Carol Steinbach, and your team for the indexes. Of all the team at Desiring God, you have known us the longest—and you are still here and willing to help. Amazing.

Noël, if we live another twenty years (till I am eighty-two and you are eighty), the marriage will be sixty years old. And judging from what I see in the Bible and my memory, it will have been a momentary marriage. But it has been so much more than momentary. It is a parable of permanence written from eternity about the greatest story that ever was. The parable is about Christ and his church. It has been a great honor to take this stage with you. What exalted roles we have been given to play! Someday I will take your hand, and stand on this stage, and make one last bow. The parable will be over, and the everlasting Reality will begin.

SCRIPTURE INDEX

PERSON INDEX

SUBJECT INDEX

❄ desiringGod

If you would like to further explore the vision of God and life presented in this book, we at Desiring God would love to serve you. We have hundreds of resources to help you grow in your passion for Jesus Christ and help you spread that passion to others. At our website, desiringGod.org, you'll find almost everything John Piper has written and preached, including more than thirty books. We've made over twenty-five years of his sermons available free online for you to read, listen to, download, and in some cases watch.

In addition, you can access hundreds of articles, find out where John Piper is speaking, learn about our conferences, discover our God-centered children's curricula, and browse our online store. John Piper receives no royalties from the books he writes and no compensation from Desiring God. The funds are all reinvested into our gospel-spreading efforts. Desiring God also has a whatever-you-can-afford policy, designed for individuals with limited discretionary funds. If you'd like more information about this policy, please contact us at the address or phone number below. We exist to help you treasure Jesus Christ and his gospel above all things because he is most glorified in you when you are most satisfied in him. Let us know how we can serve you!

Desiring God
Post Office Box 2901 Minneapolis, Minnesota 55402
888.346.4700   mail@desiringGod.org